Gates of Prayer for Assemblies

שַׁעֲרֵי תְּפִלָּה
לִכְנוּסִים

CENTRAL CONFERENCE OF AMERICAN RABBIS
5754 NEW YORK 1993

Designed by Barry Nostradamus Sher. Composed at Nostradamus Advertising by
Warren Wolfsohn. Hebrew set in NewHebrew, developed by Warren Wolfsohn
from Hadassah (Davka Corporation) and Hebraica (Linguist's Software, Inc.).

CCAR Press, 192 Lexington Avenue, New York, NY 10016   (212) 684-4990
Printed in the United States of America.
99 98 97 96 95   10 9 8 7 6 5 4 3 2

ISBN 0-88123-061-8

Contents

Preface

Gates of Prayer for Assemblies is a joint project of the Central Conference of American Rabbis and the Union of American Hebrew Congregations. It is the result of a suggestion by Rabbi Daniel H. Freelander, Director of Program for the Union of American Hebrew Congregations, and was prepared by Rabbi Freelander, Rabbi Elyse D. Frishman, and Rabbi Chaim Stern. The CCAR extends its warm gratitude to Rabbi A. Stanley Dreyfus for his meticulous copyediting of this volume and to Rabbi H. Leonard Poller, Chair of the Liturgy Committee, for editorial supervision.

This volume comes with the hope that future assemblies of the Reform Movement will benefit from having available a single book of services for Shabbat and weekdays.

The texts of the services are gender-neutral, in keeping with the recent liturgical publications of the CCAR, and are derived from *Gates of Prayer for Shabbat* and *Gates of Prayer for Weekdays*. In addition, supplementary materials come from *Gates of Prayer* itself, suitably amended, and from the soon-to-be-published *On the Doorposts of Your House: The New Union Home Prayerbook*. It should be noted that the English texts are not always translations: at times they are variations on the theme of the Hebrew; the ⸁ character indicates a *kamatz katan*, pronounced like the *o* in "often."

As we look to the future we endeavor to base ourselves on what has been best in our tradition, and we aim to add our own voice to the chorus of tradition. *Gates of Prayer for Assemblies* is a modest effort to continue on the path blazed by earlier generations of Reform Jews.

We offer *Gates of Prayer for Assemblies* in the sincere hope that it will bring all who assemble for worship, study and fellowship closer to God and to one another.

Chaim Stern
CHAPPAQUA, NEW YORK

Weekday Evening Service ערבית לחול

Your greatness, Eternal One, surpasses our understanding, and yet at times we feel Your nearness.

Overwhelmed by awe and wonder as we behold the signs of Your presence, still we feel within us a kinship with the Divine.

And so we turn to You, O God, looking at the world about us, and inward to the world within us, there to find You, and from Your presence gain life and strength.

or

God, You give meaning to our hopes, to our struggles and our strivings. Without You we are lost, our lives empty. And so when all else fails us, we turn to You! In the stillness of night, when the outer darkness enters the soul; in the press of the crowd, when we walk alone though yearning for companionship; and when in agony we are bystanders to our own confusion, we look to You for hope and peace.

God, we do not ask for a life of ease, for happiness without alloy. Instead we ask You to teach us to be uncomplaining and unafraid. In our darkness help us to find Your light, and in our loneliness to discover the many spirits akin to our own. Give us strength to face life with hope and courage, that even from its discords and conflicts we may draw blessing. Make us understand that life calls us not merely to enjoy the richness of the earth, but to exult in heights attained after the toil of climbing.

Let our darkness be dispelled by Your love, that we may rise above fear and failure, our steps sustained by faith. God, You give meaning to our lives; You are our support and our trust.

MEDITATION

There are moments when we hear the call of our higher selves, the call that links us to the Divine. Then we know how blessed we are with life and love. May this be a moment of such vision, a time of deeper attachment to the godlike in us and in our world, for which we shall give thanks and praise!

All rise

The Sh'ma and Its Blessings שמע וברכותיה

בָּרְכוּ אֶת־יי הַמְבֹרָךְ!

Praise the One to whom our praise is due!

בָּרוּךְ יי הַמְבֹרָךְ לְעוֹלָם וָעֶד!

Ba-ruch Adonai ha-m'vo-rach l'o-lam va-ed!

Praised be the One to whom our praise is due, now and for ever!

CREATION   מעריב ערבים

בָּרוּךְ אַתָּה יי, אֱלֹהֵינוּ מֶלֶךְ הָעוֹלָם,
אֲשֶׁר בִּדְבָרוֹ מַעֲרִיב עֲרָבִים, בְּחָכְמָה פּוֹתֵחַ שְׁעָרִים,
וּבִתְבוּנָה מְשַׁנֶּה עִתִּים, וּמַחֲלִיף אֶת־הַזְּמַנִּים,
וּמְסַדֵּר אֶת־הַכּוֹכָבִים בְּמִשְׁמְרוֹתֵיהֶם בָּרָקִיעַ כִּרְצוֹנוֹ.

בּוֹרֵא יוֹם וָלָיְלָה, גּוֹלֵל אוֹר מִפְּנֵי חְשֶׁךְ וְחְשֶׁךְ מִפְּנֵי אוֹר,
וּמַעֲבִיר יוֹם וּמֵבִיא לָיְלָה, וּמַבְדִּיל בֵּין יוֹם וּבֵין לָיְלָה,
יי צְבָאוֹת שְׁמוֹ. אֵל חַי וְקַיָּם, תָּמִיד יִמְלוֹךְ עָלֵינוּ
לְעוֹלָם וָעֶד. בָּרוּךְ אַתָּה יי, הַמַּעֲרִיב עֲרָבִים.

We praise You, Eternal God, Sovereign of the universe, whose word brings on the evening, whose wisdom opens heaven's gates, whose understanding makes the ages pass and the seasons alternate, and whose will controls the stars as they travel through the skies.

2

You are Creator of day and night, rolling light away from dark-
ness, and darkness from light. You cause day to pass and bring on
the night, separating day from night. You command the Hosts of
heaven! May the living and eternal God rule us always, to the end
of time! We praise You, O God, whose word makes evening fall.

REVELATION   אהבת עולם

אַהֲבַת עוֹלָם בֵּית יִשְׂרָאֵל עַמְּךָ אָהַבְתָּ.

תּוֹרָה וּמִצְוֹת, חֻקִּים וּמִשְׁפָּטִים אוֹתָנוּ לִמַּדְתָּ.

עַל־כֵּן, יי אֱלֹהֵינוּ, בְּשָׁכְבֵּנוּ וּבְקוּמֵנוּ נָשִׂיחַ בְּחֻקֶּיךָ,

וְנִשְׂמַח בְּדִבְרֵי תוֹרָתֶךָ וּבְמִצְוֹתֶיךָ לְעוֹלָם וָעֶד.

כִּי הֵם חַיֵּינוּ וְאֹרֶךְ יָמֵינוּ, וּבָהֶם נֶהְגֶּה יוֹמָם וָלָיְלָה.

וְאַהֲבָתְךָ אַל־תָּסוּר מִמֶּנּוּ לְעוֹלָמִים!

בָּרוּךְ אַתָּה יי, אוֹהֵב עַמּוֹ יִשְׂרָאֵל.

Unending is Your love for Your people, the House of Israel:
Torah and Mitzvot, laws and precepts have You taught us.

Therefore, O God, when we lie down and when we rise up,
we will meditate on Your laws
and rejoice in Your Torah and Mitzvot for ever.

Day and night we will reflect on them,
for they are our life and the length of our days.
Then Your love shall never depart from our hearts!
We praise You, O God: You love Your people Israel.

❖ ❖

3

שְׁמַע יִשְׂרָאֵל: יהוה אֱלֹהֵינוּ, יהוה אֶחָד!

Sh'ma Yis-ra-eil: Adonai Eh-lo-hei-nu, Adonai Eh-chad!

Hear, O Israel: the Eternal One is our God,
the Eternal God alone!

בָּרוּךְ שֵׁם כְּבוֹד מַלְכוּתוֹ לְעוֹלָם וָעֶד!

Ba-ruch sheim k'vod mal-chu-toh l'o-lam va-ed!

Blessed is God's glorious majesty for ever and ever!

All are seated

וְאָהַבְתָּ אֵת יהוה אֱלֹהֶיךָ בְּכָל־לְבָבְךָ וּבְכָל־נַפְשְׁךָ
וּבְכָל־מְאֹדֶךָ: וְהָיוּ הַדְּבָרִים הָאֵלֶּה אֲשֶׁר אָנֹכִי מְצַוְּךָ
הַיּוֹם עַל־לְבָבֶךָ: וְשִׁנַּנְתָּם לְבָנֶיךָ וְדִבַּרְתָּ בָּם בְּשִׁבְתְּךָ
בְּבֵיתֶךָ וּבְלֶכְתְּךָ בַדֶּרֶךְ וּבְשָׁכְבְּךָ וּבְקוּמֶךָ: וּקְשַׁרְתָּם
לְאוֹת עַל־יָדֶךָ וְהָיוּ לְטֹטָפֹת בֵּין עֵינֶיךָ: וּכְתַבְתָּם
עַל־מְזֻזוֹת בֵּיתֶךָ וּבִשְׁעָרֶיךָ:

לְמַעַן תִּזְכְּרוּ וַעֲשִׂיתֶם אֶת־כָּל־מִצְוֹתָי וִהְיִיתֶם קְדֹשִׁים
לֵאלֹהֵיכֶם: אֲנִי יהוה אֱלֹהֵיכֶם אֲשֶׁר הוֹצֵאתִי אֶתְכֶם
מֵאֶרֶץ מִצְרַיִם לִהְיוֹת לָכֶם לֵאלֹהִים. אֲנִי יהוה אֱלֹהֵיכֶם:

V'a-hav-ta et Adonai Eh-lo-heh-cha
b'chol l'va-v'cha u-v'chol naf-sh'cha u-v'chol m'o-deh-cha.
V'ha-yu ha-d'va-rim ha-ei-leh
a-sher a-no-chi m'tza-v'cha ha-yom al l'va-veh-cha.
V'shi-nan-tam l'va-neh-cha v'di-bar-ta bam
b'shiv-t'cha b'vei-teh-cha u-v'lech-t'cha va-deh-rech
u-v'shoch-b'cha u-v'ku-meh-cha. U-k'shar-tam l'oht al ya-deh-cha
v'ha-yu l'toh-ta-foht bein ei-neh-cha;
uch'tav-tam al m'zu-zoht bei-teh-cha u-vi-sh'a-reh-cha.

4

L'ma-an tiz-k'ru va-a-si-tem et kol mitz-vo-tai,
vi-h'yi-tem k'doh-shim lei-lo-hei-chem.
A-ni Adonai Eh-lo-hei-chem
a-sher ho-tzei-ti et-chem mei-eh-retz mitz-ra-yim
li-h'yoht la-chem lei-lo-him.
A-ni Adonai Eh-lo-hei-chem.

You shall love the Eternal One, your God, with all your heart, with all your mind, with all your being. Set these words, which I command you this day, upon your heart. Teach them faithfully to your children; speak of them in your home and on your way, when you lie down and when you rise up. Bind them as a sign upon your hand; let them be a symbol before your eyes; inscribe them on the doorposts of your house, and on your gates.

Be mindful of all My Mitzvot, and do them:
so shall you consecrate yourselves to your God.
I am your Eternal God who led you out of Egypt to be your
God; I am your Eternal God.

REDEMPTION   גאולה

All this we hold to be true and sure: You alone are our God;
there is none else, and we are Israel Your people.

You are our Sovereign: You deliver us from the hand of
oppressors, and save us from the fist of tyrants.

You do wonders without number,
marvels that pass our understanding.

You give us our life;
by Your help we survive all who seek our destruction.

You did wonders for us in the land of Egypt,
miracles and marvels in the land of Pharaoh.

You led Your people Israel out, forever to serve You in freedom.

When Your children witnessed Your power, they extolled You
and gave You thanks; willingly they enthroned You; and, full of
joy, Moses, Miriam and all Israel sang this song:

5

מִי־כָמֹכָה בָּאֵלִם, יהוה? מִי כָּמֹכָה, נֶאְדָּר בַּקֹּדֶשׁ,
נוֹרָא תְהִלֹת, עֹשֵׂה פֶלֶא?

מַלְכוּתְךָ רָאוּ בָנֶיךָ, בּוֹקֵעַ יָם לִפְנֵי מֹשֶׁה; זֶה אֵלִי!
עָנוּ וְאָמְרוּ: יהוה יִמְלֹךְ לְעֹלָם וָעֶד!

וְנֶאֱמַר: כִּי פָדָה יי אֶת־יַעֲקֹב, וּגְאָלוֹ מִיַּד חָזָק מִמֶּנּוּ.
בָּרוּךְ אַתָּה יי, גָּאַל יִשְׂרָאֵל.

Mi cha-mo-cha ba-ei-lim, Adonai?
Mi ka-mo-cha, neh-dar ba-ko-desh, no-ra t'hi-loht, o-sei feh-leh?

Mal-chu-t'cha ra-u va-neh-cha, bo-kei-a yam li-f'nei Mo-sheh;
zeh Ei-li! A-nu v'a-m'ru: Adonai yim-loch l'o-lam va-ed.

V'neh-eh-mar: Ki fa-da Adonai et Ya-a-kov,
u-g'a-lo mi-yad cha-zak mi-meh-nu.
Ba-ruch a-ta Adonai, ga-al Yis-ra-eil.

Who is like You, Eternal One, among the gods that are worshipped?
Who is like You, majestic in holiness, awesome in splendor, doing
wonders?

In their escape from the sea, Your children saw Your sovereign might
displayed. "This is my God!" they cried. "The Eternal will reign
for ever and ever!"

And it has been said: The Eternal One delivered Jacob, and redeemed
us from the hand of one stronger than ourselves.

We praise You, Eternal One, Redeemer of Israel.

6

DIVINE PROVIDENCE   הַשְׁכִּיבֵנוּ

הַשְׁכִּיבֵנוּ, יי אֱלֹהֵינוּ, לְשָׁלוֹם, וְהַעֲמִידֵנוּ, מַלְכֵּנוּ, לְחַיִּים.
וּפְרוֹשׂ עָלֵינוּ סֻכַּת שְׁלוֹמֶךָ, וְתַקְּנֵנוּ בְּעֵצָה טוֹבָה מִלְּפָנֶיךָ,
וְהוֹשִׁיעֵנוּ לְמַעַן שְׁמֶךָ, וְהָגֵן בַּעֲדֵנוּ. וְהָסֵר מֵעָלֵינוּ אוֹיֵב,
דֶּבֶר וְחֶרֶב וְרָעָב וְיָגוֹן; וְהָסֵר שָׂטָן מִלְּפָנֵינוּ וּמֵאַחֲרֵינוּ,
וּבְצֵל כְּנָפֶיךָ תַּסְתִּירֵנוּ, כִּי אֵל שׁוֹמְרֵנוּ וּמַצִּילֵנוּ אָתָּה,
כִּי אֵל מֶלֶךְ חַנּוּן וְרַחוּם אָתָּה. וּשְׁמוֹר צֵאתֵנוּ וּבוֹאֵנוּ
לְחַיִּים וּלְשָׁלוֹם, מֵעַתָּה וְעַד עוֹלָם.
בָּרוּךְ אַתָּה יי, שׁוֹמֵר עַמּוֹ יִשְׂרָאֵל לָעַד.

Grant that we may lie down in peace, Eternal God, and raise us up, O Sovereign, to life renewed. Spread over us the shelter of Your peace; guide us with Your good counsel; and for Your name's sake, be our Help.

Shield us from hatred and plague; keep us from war and famine and anguish; subdue our inclination to evil. O God, our Guardian and Helper, our gracious and merciful Ruler, give us refuge in the shadow of Your wings. O guard our coming and our going, that now and always we have life and peace.

We praise You, Eternal One, the Guardian of Israel.

All rise

7

READER'S KADDISH   חצי קדיש

יִתְגַּדַּל וְיִתְקַדַּשׁ שְׁמֵהּ רַבָּא בְּעָלְמָא דִי־בְרָא כִרְעוּתֵהּ,
וְיַמְלִיךְ מַלְכוּתֵהּ בְּחַיֵּיכוֹן וּבְיוֹמֵיכוֹן וּבְחַיֵּי דְכָל־בֵּית
יִשְׂרָאֵל, בַּעֲגָלָא וּבִזְמַן קָרִיב, וְאִמְרוּ: אָמֵן.

יְהֵא שְׁמֵהּ רַבָּא מְבָרַךְ לְעָלַם וּלְעָלְמֵי עָלְמַיָּא.

יִתְבָּרַךְ וְיִשְׁתַּבַּח, וְיִתְפָּאַר וְיִתְרוֹמַם וְיִתְנַשֵּׂא, וְיִתְהַדָּר
וְיִתְעַלֶּה וְיִתְהַלָּל שְׁמֵהּ דְּקוּדְשָׁא, בְּרִיךְ הוּא, לְעֵלָּא
מִן־כָּל־בִּרְכָתָא וְשִׁירָתָא, תֻּשְׁבְּחָתָא וְנֶחֱמָתָא
דַּאֲמִירָן בְּעָלְמָא, וְאִמְרוּ: אָמֵן.

Yit-ga-dal v'yit-ka-dash sh'mei ra-ba b'al-ma di-v'ra chir-u-tei,
v'yam-lich mal-chu-tei b'cha-yei-chon u-v'yo-mei-chon u-v'cha-yei
d'chol beit Yis-ra-eil, ba-a-ga-la u-viz-man ka-riv, v'i-m'ru: A-mein.

Y'hei sh'mei ra-ba m'va-rach l'a-lam u-l'al-mei al-ma-ya.

Yit-ba-rach v'yish-ta-bach v'yit-pa-ar, v'yit-ro-mam, v'yit-na-sei,
v'yit-ha-dar, v'yit-a-leh, v'yit-ha-lal sh'mei d'kud-sha, b'rich hu,
l'ei-la min kol bir-cha-ta v'shi-ra-ta, tush-b'cha-ta v'neh-cheh-ma-ta
da-a-mi-ran b'al-ma, v'i-m'ru: A-mein.

The Weekday T'filah is on page 21

Weekday Morning Service שַׁחֲרִית לְחוֹל

בָּרְכִי נַפְשִׁי אֶת יְיָ! יְיָ אֱלֹהַי, גָּדַלְתָּ מְּאֹד!
הוֹד וְהָדָר לָבָשְׁתָּ, עֹטֶה אוֹר כַּשַּׂלְמָה, נוֹטֶה שָׁמַיִם כַּיְרִיעָה.

Praise the Eternal One, O my soul!
O God, You are very great!
Arrayed in glory and majesty, You wrap Yourself in light as
with a garment, You stretch out the heavens like a curtain.

בָּרוּךְ אַתָּה יְיָ, אֱלֹהֵינוּ מֶלֶךְ הָעוֹלָם,
אֲשֶׁר קִדְּשָׁנוּ בְּמִצְוֹתָיו וְצִוָּנוּ לְהִתְעַטֵּף בַּצִּיצִת.

We praise You, Eternal God, Sovereign of the universe:
You hallow us with Your Mitzvot,
and teach us to wrap ourselves in the fringed Tallit.

9

Morning Blessings ברכות השחר

FOR THE BLESSING OF WORSHIP מה טבו

מַה־טֹּבוּ אֹהָלֶיךָ, יַעֲקֹב, מִשְׁכְּנֹתֶיךָ, יִשְׂרָאֵל.

וַאֲנִי, בְּרֹב חַסְדְּךָ אָבֹא בֵיתֶךָ,
אֶשְׁתַּחֲוֶה אֶל־הֵיכַל קָדְשְׁךָ בְּיִרְאָתֶךָ.

יהוה, אָהַבְתִּי מְעוֹן בֵּיתֶךָ, וּמְקוֹם מִשְׁכַּן כְּבוֹדֶךָ.
וַאֲנִי אֶשְׁתַּחֲוֶה וְאֶכְרָעָה, אֶבְרְכָה לִפְנֵי־יהוה עֹשִׂי.

וַאֲנִי תְפִלָּתִי לְךָ, יהוה, עֵת רָצוֹן.
אֱלֹהִים בְּרָב־חַסְדֶּךָ, עֲנֵנִי בֶּאֱמֶת יִשְׁעֶךָ.

Mah to-vu o-ha-leh-cha Ya-a-kov, mish-k'no-teh-cha, Yis-ra-eil!

Va-a-ni, b'rov chas-d'cha a-vo vei-teh-cha,
esh-ta-cha-veh el hei-chal kod-sh'cha b'-yir-a-teh-cha.

Adonai a-hav-ti m'on bei-te-cha u-m'kom mish-kan k'vo-deh-cha.
Va-a-ni esh-ta-cha-veh v'ech-ra-ah, ev-r'chah li-f'nei Adonai o-si.

Va-a-ni t'fi-la-ti l'cha Adonai eit ra-tson.
Eh-lo-him b'rov chas-deh-cha a-nei-ni beh-eh-met yish-eh-cha.

How lovely are Your tents, O Jacob, your dwelling-places, O Israel!

As for me, O God abounding in grace,
I enter Your house to worship with awe in Your sacred place.

I love Your house, Eternal One, the dwelling-place of Your glory;
humbly I worship You, humbly I seek blessing from God my Maker.

To You, Eternal One, goes my prayer: may this be a time of Your
favor. In Your great love, O God, answer me with Your saving truth.

FOR HEALTH   אשר יצר

בָּרוּךְ אַתָּה יי, אֱלֹהֵינוּ מֶלֶךְ הָעוֹלָם, אֲשֶׁר יָצַר
אֶת־הָאָדָם בְּחָכְמָה, וּבָרָא בוֹ נְקָבִים נְקָבִים, חֲלוּלִים
חֲלוּלִים. גָּלוּי וְיָדְוּעַ לִפְנֵי כִסֵּא כְבוֹדֶךָ, שֶׁאִם יִפָּתֵחַ אֶחָד
מֵהֶם, אוֹ יִסָּתֵם אֶחָד מֵהֶם, אִי אֶפְשָׁר לְהִתְקַיֵּם וְלַעֲמוֹד
לְפָנֶיךָ. בָּרוּךְ אַתָּה יי, רוֹפֵא כָל־בָּשָׂר וּמַפְלִיא לַעֲשׂוֹת.

*We praise You, Eternal God, Sovereign of the universe:
With divine wisdom You have made our bodies, combining veins,
arteries, and vital organs into a finely balanced network.*

*Wondrous Maker and Sustainer of life, were one of them to fail —
how well we are aware! — we would lack the strength to stand in
life before You.*

Source of our health and strength, we give You thanks and praise.

FOR TORAH   לעסוק בדברי תורה

בָּרוּךְ אַתָּה יי, אֱלֹהֵינוּ מֶלֶךְ הָעוֹלָם, אֲשֶׁר קִדְּשָׁנוּ בְּמִצְוֹתָיו
וְצִוָּנוּ לַעֲסוֹק בְּדִבְרֵי תוֹרָה.

*We praise You, Eternal God, Sovereign of the universe: You hallow
us with the gift of Torah and invite us to immerse ourselves in its
words.*

*Eternal our God, make the words of Your Torah sweet to us, and to
the House of Israel, Your people, that we and our children may be
lovers of Your name and students of Your Torah. We praise You, O
God, Teacher of Torah to Your people Israel.*

אֵלּוּ דְבָרִים שֶׁאֵין לָהֶם שִׁעוּר, שֶׁאָדָם אוֹכֵל פֵּרוֹתֵיהֶם
בָּעוֹלָם הַזֶּה וְהַקֶּרֶן קַיֶּמֶת לוֹ לָעוֹלָם הַבָּא, וְאֵלּוּ הֵן:

These are obligations without measure, whose reward too, is
without measure:

To honor father and mother;	כִּבּוּד אָב וָאֵם,
to perform acts of love and kindness;	וּגְמִילוּת חֲסָדִים,
to attend the house of study daily;	וְהַשְׁכָּמַת בֵּית הַמִּדְרָשׁ
	שַׁחֲרִית וְעַרְבִית,
to welcome the stranger;	וְהַכְנָסַת אוֹרְחִים,
to visit the sick;	וּבִקּוּר חוֹלִים,
to rejoice with bride and groom;	וְהַכְנָסַת כַּלָּה,
to console the bereaved;	וּלְוָיַת הַמֵּת,
to pray with sincerity;	וְעִיּוּן תְּפִלָּה,
to make peace when there is strife.	וַהֲבָאַת שָׁלוֹם
	בֵּין אָדָם לַחֲבֵרוֹ;

וְתַלְמוּד תּוֹרָה כְּנֶגֶד כֻּלָּם.

And the study of Torah leads to them all.

FOR THE SOUL   אלהי נשמה

אֱלֹהַי, נְשָׁמָה שֶׁנָּתַתָּ בִּי טְהוֹרָה הִיא! אַתָּה בְרָאתָהּ,
אַתָּה יְצַרְתָּהּ, אַתָּה נְפַחְתָּהּ בִּי, וְאַתָּה מְשַׁמְּרָהּ בְּקִרְבִּי.
כָּל־זְמַן שֶׁהַנְּשָׁמָה בְּקִרְבִּי, מוֹדֶה אֲנִי לְפָנֶיךָ, יי אֱלֹהַי
וֵאלֹהֵי אֲבוֹתַי וְאִמּוֹתַי, רִבּוֹן כָּל־הַמַּעֲשִׂים, אֲדוֹן
כָּל־הַנְּשָׁמוֹת.
בָּרוּךְ אַתָּה יי, אֲשֶׁר בְּיָדוֹ נֶפֶשׁ כָּל־חָי, וְרוּחַ כָּל־בְּשַׂר־אִישׁ.

The soul that You have given me, O God, is pure! You created and
formed it, breathed it into me, and within me You sustain it. So

12 ✓

long as I have breath, therefore, I will give thanks to You, my God and God of all ages, Source of all being, loving Guide of every human spirit.

We praise You, O God, in whose hands are the souls of all the living and the spirits of all flesh.

FOR OUR BLESSINGS　　　　　　　　　　　　　　　　　נסים בכל יום

בָּרוּךְ אַתָּה יי, אֱלֹהֵינוּ מֶלֶךְ הָעוֹלָם,
אֲשֶׁר נָתַן לַשֶּׂכְוִי בִינָה לְהַבְחִין בֵּין יוֹם וּבֵין לָיְלָה.

We praise You, Eternal God, Sovereign of the universe:
You have implanted mind and instinct within every living being.

בָּרוּךְ אַתָּה יי, אֱלֹהֵינוּ מֶלֶךְ הָעוֹלָם, שֶׁעָשַׂנִי יִשְׂרָאֵל.

Praised be the Eternal God, who has made me a Jew.

בָּרוּךְ אַתָּה יי, אֱלֹהֵינוּ מֶלֶךְ הָעוֹלָם, שֶׁעָשַׂנִי בֶּן חוֹרִין.

Praised be the Eternal God, who has made me to be free.

בָּרוּךְ אַתָּה יי, אֱלֹהֵינוּ מֶלֶךְ הָעוֹלָם, פּוֹקֵחַ עִוְרִים.

Praised be the Eternal God, who helps the blind to see.

בָּרוּךְ אַתָּה יי, אֱלֹהֵינוּ מֶלֶךְ הָעוֹלָם, מַלְבִּישׁ עֲרֻמִּים.

Praised be the Eternal God, who clothes the naked.

בָּרוּךְ אַתָּה יי, אֱלֹהֵינוּ מֶלֶךְ הָעוֹלָם, מַתִּיר אֲסוּרִים.

Praised be the Eternal God, who frees the captive.

בָּרוּךְ אַתָּה יי, אֱלֹהֵינוּ מֶלֶךְ הָעוֹלָם, זוֹקֵף כְּפוּפִים.

Praised be the Eternal God, who lifts up the fallen.

בָּרוּךְ אַתָּה יי, אֱלֹהֵינוּ מֶלֶךְ הָעוֹלָם, הַמֵּכִין מִצְעֲדֵי־גָבֶר.

Praised be the Eternal God, who makes firm our steps.

13

בָּרוּךְ אַתָּה יי, אֱלֹהֵינוּ מֶלֶךְ הָעוֹלָם, אוֹזֵר יִשְׂרָאֵל בִּגְבוּרָה.

Praised be the Eternal God,
who girds our people Israel with strength.

בָּרוּךְ אַתָּה יי, אֱלֹהֵינוּ מֶלֶךְ הָעוֹלָם,
עוֹטֵר יִשְׂרָאֵל בְּתִפְאָרָה.

Praised be the Eternal God, who crowns Israel with glory.

בָּרוּךְ אַתָּה יי, אֱלֹהֵינוּ מֶלֶךְ הָעוֹלָם, הַנּוֹתֵן לַיָּעֵף כֹּחַ.

Praised be the Eternal God, who gives strength to the weary.

בָּרוּךְ אַתָּה יי, אֱלֹהֵינוּ מֶלֶךְ הָעוֹלָם,
הַמַּעֲבִיר שֵׁנָה מֵעֵינָי וּתְנוּמָה מֵעַפְעַפָּי.

Praised be the Eternal God,
who removes sleep from the eyes, slumber from the eyelids.

FOR CONSCIENCE   תורה ומצוות

Eternal One, our God and God of all ages,
school us in Your Torah and bind us to Your Mitzvot.

Help us to keep far from sin, to master temptation, and to avoid
falling under its spell. May our darker passions not rule us, nor
evil companions lead us astray.

Strengthen in us the voice of conscience; prompt us to deeds of
goodness; and bend our every impulse to Your service, so that
this day and always we may know Your love and the good will
of all who behold us. We praise You, O God: You bestow love
and kindness on Your people Israel.

❖ ❖

At all times let us revere God inwardly as well as outwardly,
acknowledge the truth and speak it in our hearts.

14 ✓

All rise

READER'S KADDISH   חצי קדיש

יִתְגַּדַּל וְיִתְקַדַּשׁ שְׁמֵהּ רַבָּא בְּעָלְמָא דִּי־בְרָא כִרְעוּתֵהּ,
וְיַמְלִיךְ מַלְכוּתֵהּ בְּחַיֵּיכוֹן וּבְיוֹמֵיכוֹן וּבְחַיֵּי דְכָל־בֵּית
יִשְׂרָאֵל, בַּעֲגָלָא וּבִזְמַן קָרִיב, וְאִמְרוּ: אָמֵן.

יְהֵא שְׁמֵהּ רַבָּא מְבָרַךְ לְעָלַם וּלְעָלְמֵי עָלְמַיָּא.

יִתְבָּרַךְ וְיִשְׁתַּבַּח, וְיִתְפָּאַר וְיִתְרוֹמַם וְיִתְנַשֵּׂא, וְיִתְהַדָּר
וְיִתְעַלֶּה וְיִתְהַלַּל שְׁמֵהּ דְּקוּדְשָׁא, בְּרִיךְ הוּא, לְעֵלָּא
מִן־כָּל־בִּרְכָתָא וְשִׁירָתָא, תֻּשְׁבְּחָתָא וְנֶחֱמָתָא
דַּאֲמִירָן בְּעָלְמָא, וְאִמְרוּ: אָמֵן.

Yit-ga-dal v'yit-ka-dash sh'mei ra-ba b'al-ma di-v'ra chir-u-tei,
v'yam-lich mal-chu-tei b'cha-yei-chon u-v'yo-mei-chon u-v'cha-yei
d'chol beit Yis-ra-eil, ba-a-ga-la u-viz-man ka-riv, v'i-m'ru: A-mein.

Y'hei sh'mei ra-ba m'va-rach l'a-lam u-l'al-mei al-ma-ya.

Yit-ba-rach v'yish-ta-bach v'yit-pa-ar, v'yit-ro-mam, v'yit-na-sei,
v'yit-ha-dar, v'yit-a-leh, v'yit-ha-lal sh'mei d'kud-sha, b'rich hu,
l'ei-la min kol bir-cha-ta v'shi-ra-ta, tush-b'cha-ta v'neh-cheh-ma-ta
da-a-mi-ran b'al-ma, v'i-m'ru: A-mein.

The Sh'ma and Its Blessings שמע וברכותיה

בָּרְכוּ אֶת־יי הַמְבֹרָךְ!

Praise the One to whom our praise is due!

בָּרוּךְ יי הַמְבֹרָךְ לְעוֹלָם וָעֶד!

Ba-ruch Adonai ha-m'vo-rach l'o-lam va-ed!

Praised be the One to whom our praise is due, now and for ever!

15

CREATION   יוֹצֵר

בָּרוּךְ אַתָּה יי, אֱלֹהֵינוּ מֶלֶךְ הָעוֹלָם, יוֹצֵר אוֹר וּבוֹרֵא
חְשֶׁךְ, עֹשֶׂה שָׁלוֹם וּבוֹרֵא אֶת־הַכֹּל. הַמֵּאִיר לָאָרֶץ
וְלַדָּרִים עָלֶיהָ בְּרַחֲמִים, וּבְטוּבוֹ מְחַדֵּשׁ בְּכָל־יוֹם תָּמִיד
מַעֲשֵׂה בְרֵאשִׁית. מָה רַבּוּ מַעֲשֶׂיךָ, יי! כֻּלָּם בְּחָכְמָה עָשִׂיתָ,
מָלְאָה הָאָרֶץ קִנְיָנֶךָ. תִּתְבָּרַךְ, יי אֱלֹהֵינוּ, עַל־שֶׁבַח מַעֲשֵׂה
יָדֶיךָ, וְעַל־מְאוֹרֵי־אוֹר שֶׁעָשִׂיתָ: יְפָאֲרוּךָ. סֶלָה.
בָּרוּךְ אַתָּה יי, יוֹצֵר הַמְּאוֹרוֹת.

*We praise You, Eternal God, Soverign of the universe, whose
mercy makes light to shine over the earth and all its inhabitants,
and whose goodness renews day by day the work of creation.*

*How manifold are Your works, O God! In wisdom You have made
them all. The heavens declare Your glory. The earth reveals Your
creative power. You form light and darkness, bring harmony into
nature, and peace to the human heart.*

We praise You, O God, Creator of light.

REVELATION   אהבה רבה

אַהֲבָה רַבָּה אֲהַבְתָּנוּ, יי אֱלֹהֵינוּ, חֶמְלָה גְדוֹלָה וִיתֵרָה
חָמַלְתָּ עָלֵינוּ. אָבִינוּ מַלְכֵּנוּ, בַּעֲבוּר אֲבוֹתֵינוּ וְאִמּוֹתֵינוּ
שֶׁבָּטְחוּ בְךָ וַתְּלַמְּדֵם חֻקֵּי חַיִּים, כֵּן תְּחָנֵּנוּ וּתְלַמְּדֵנוּ.
אָבִינוּ, הָאָב הָרַחֲמָן, הַמְרַחֵם, רַחֵם עָלֵינוּ וְתֵן בְּלִבֵּנוּ
לְהָבִין וּלְהַשְׂכִּיל, לִשְׁמֹעַ לִלְמֹד וּלְלַמֵּד, לִשְׁמֹר וְלַעֲשׂוֹת
וּלְקַיֵּם אֶת־כָּל־דִּבְרֵי תַלְמוּד תּוֹרָתֶךָ בְּאַהֲבָה.
וְהָאֵר עֵינֵינוּ בְּתוֹרָתֶךָ, וְדַבֵּק לִבֵּנוּ בְּמִצְוֹתֶיךָ, וְיַחֵד לְבָבֵנוּ
לְאַהֲבָה וּלְיִרְאָה אֶת־שְׁמֶךָ. וְלֹא־נֵבוֹשׁ לְעוֹלָם וָעֶד,
כִּי בְשֵׁם קָדְשְׁךָ הַגָּדוֹל וְהַנּוֹרָא בָּטָחְנוּ. נָגִילָה וְנִשְׂמְחָה
בִּישׁוּעָתֶךָ, כִּי אֵל פּוֹעֵל יְשׁוּעוֹת אָתָּה, וּבָנוּ בָחַרְתָּ וְקֵרַבְתָּנוּ

לְשִׁמְךָ הַגָּדוֹל סֶלָה בֶּאֱמֶת, לְהוֹדוֹת לְךָ וּלְיַחֶדְךָ בְּאַהֲבָה.
בָּרוּךְ אַתָּה יי, הַבּוֹחֵר בְּעַמּוֹ יִשְׂרָאֵל בְּאַהֲבָה.

Deep is Your love for us, abiding Your compassion. From of old we have put our trust in You, and You have taught us the laws of life. Be gracious now to us, that we may understand and fulfill the teachings of Your word.

Enlighten our eyes in Your Torah, that we may cling to Your Mitzvot. Unite our hearts to love and revere Your name.

We trust in You and rejoice in Your saving power, for You are the Source of our help. You have called us and drawn us near to You in faithfulness.

Joyfully we lift up our voices and proclaim Your unity, O God. In love, You have called us to Your service!

❖ ❖

שְׁמַע יִשְׂרָאֵל: יהוה אֱלֹהֵינוּ, יהוה אֶחָד!

Sh'ma Yis-ra-eil: Adonai Eh-lo-hei-nu, Adonai Eh-chad!

Hear, O Israel: the Eternal One is our God,
the Eternal God alone!

בָּרוּךְ שֵׁם כְּבוֹד מַלְכוּתוֹ לְעוֹלָם וָעֶד!

Ba-ruch sheim k'vod mal-chu-toh l'o-lam va-ed!

Blessed is God's glorious majesty for ever and ever!

All are seated

וְאָהַבְתָּ אֵת יְהֹוָה אֱלֹהֶיךָ בְּכָל־לְבָבְךָ וּבְכָל־נַפְשְׁךָ
וּבְכָל־מְאֹדֶךָ: וְהָיוּ הַדְּבָרִים הָאֵלֶּה אֲשֶׁר אָנֹכִי מְצַוְּךָ
הַיּוֹם עַל־לְבָבֶךָ: וְשִׁנַּנְתָּם לְבָנֶיךָ וְדִבַּרְתָּ בָּם בְּשִׁבְתְּךָ
בְּבֵיתֶךָ וּבְלֶכְתְּךָ בַדֶּרֶךְ וּבְשָׁכְבְּךָ וּבְקוּמֶךָ: וּקְשַׁרְתָּם

17 √

לְאוֹת עַל־יָדֶךָ וְהָיוּ לְטֹטָפֹת בֵּין עֵינֶיךָ: וּכְתַבְתָּם
עַל־מְזֻזֹת בֵּיתֶךָ וּבִשְׁעָרֶיךָ:

לְמַעַן תִּזְכְּרוּ וַעֲשִׂיתֶם אֶת־כָּל־מִצְוֹתָי וִהְיִיתֶם קְדֹשִׁים
לֵאלֹהֵיכֶם: אֲנִי יְהֹוָה אֱלֹהֵיכֶם אֲשֶׁר הוֹצֵאתִי אֶתְכֶם
מֵאֶרֶץ מִצְרַיִם לִהְיוֹת לָכֶם לֵאלֹהִים אֲנִי יְהֹוָה אֱלֹהֵיכֶם:

V'a-hav-ta et Adonai Eh-lo-heh-cha
b'chol l'va-v'cha u-v'chol naf-sh'cha u-v'chol m'o-deh-cha.
V'ha-yu ha-d'va-rim ha-ei-leh
a-sher a-no-chi m'tza-v'cha ha-yom al l'va-veh-cha.
V'shi-nan-tam l'va-neh-cha v'di-bar-ta bam
b'shiv-t'cha b'vei-teh-cha u-v'lech-t'cha va-deh-rech
u-v'shoch-b'cha u-v'ku-meh-cha. U-k'shar-tam l'oht al ya-deh-cha
v'ha-yu l'toh-ta-foht bein ei-neh-cha;
uch'tav-tam al m'zu-zoht bei-teh-cha u-vi-sh'a-reh-cha.

L'ma-an tiz-k'ru va-a-si-tem et kol mitz-vo-tai,
vi-h'yi-tem k'doh-shim lei-lo-hei-chem.
A-ni Adonai Eh-lo-hei-chem
a-sher ho-tzei-ti et-chem mei-eh-retz mitz-ra-yim
li-h'yoht la-chem lei-lo-him.
A-ni Adonai Eh-lo-hei-chem.

You shall love the Eternal One, your God, with all your heart, with all your mind, with all your being. Set these words, which I command you this day, upon your heart. Teach them faithfully to your children; speak of them in your home and on your way, when you lie down and when you rise up. Bind them as a sign upon your hand; let them be a symbol before your eyes; inscribe them on the doorposts of your house, and on your gates.

*Be mindful of all My Mitzvot, and do them:
so shall you consecrate yourselves to your God.
I am your Eternal God who led you out of
Egypt to be your God; I am your Eternal God.*

REDEMPTION   גאולה

Eternal truth it is that You alone are God,
and there is none else.
May the righteous of all nations rejoice in Your love
and exult in Your justice.

Let them beat their swords into plowshares;
let them beat their spears into pruninghooks.

Let nation not lift up sword against nation;
let them study war no more.
You shall not hate another in your heart;
you shall love your neighbor as yourself.

Let the stranger in your midst be to you as the native;
for you were strangers in the land of Egypt.
From the house of bondage we went forth to freedom;
so let all be free to sing with joy:

מִי־כָמֹכָה בָּאֵלִם, יהוה? מִי כָּמֹכָה, נֶאְדָּר בַּקֹּדֶשׁ,
נוֹרָא תְהִלֹּת, עֹשֵׂה פֶלֶא?

שִׁירָה חֲדָשָׁה שִׁבְּחוּ גְאוּלִים לְשִׁמְךָ עַל־שְׂפַת הַיָּם;
יַחַד כֻּלָּם הוֹדוּ וְהִמְלִיכוּ וְאָמְרוּ: יי יִמְלֹךְ לְעוֹלָם וָעֶד!

צוּר יִשְׂרָאֵל, קוּמָה בְּעֶזְרַת יִשְׂרָאֵל,
וּפְדֵה כִנְאֻמֶךָ יְהוּדָה וְיִשְׂרָאֵל.
גֹּאֲלֵנוּ יי צְבָאוֹת שְׁמוֹ, קְדוֹשׁ יִשְׂרָאֵל.
בָּרוּךְ אַתָּה יי, גָּאַל יִשְׂרָאֵל.

Mi cha-mo-cha ba-ei-lim, Adonai?
Mi ka-mo-cha, neh-dar ba-ko-desh,
no-ra t'hi-loht, o-sei feh-leh?

19 ✓

Shi-ra cha-da-sha shi-b'chu g'u-lim l'shi-m'cha al s'fat ha-yam;
ya-chad ku-lam ho-du v'him-li-chu v'a-m'ru:
Adonai yim-loch l'o-lam va-ed!

Tsur Yis-ra-eil, ku-ma b'ez-rat Yis-ra-eil,
u-f'dei chi-n'u-me-cha Y'hu-dah v'yis-ra-eil.

Go-a-lei-nu Adonai ts'va-ot sh'mo,
k'dosh Yis-ra-eil.
Ba-ruch a-tah, Adonai, ga-al Yis-ra-eil.

Who is like You, Eternal One, among the gods that are worshipped? Who is like You, majestic in holiness, awesome in splendor, doing wonders?

A new song the redeemed sang to Your name. At the shore of the sea, saved from destruction, they proclaimed Your sovereign power: The Eternal One will reign for ever and ever!

O Rock of Israel, come to Israel's help. Fulfill Your promise of redemption for Judah and Israel. Our Redeemer is God on High, the Holy One of Israel. We praise You, Eternal One, Redeemer of Israel.

The Weekday T'filah is on page 21

Weekday T'filah   תפלה לימות החול

All rise

אֲדֹנָי, שְׂפָתַי תִּפְתָּח וּפִי יַגִּיד תְּהִלָּתֶךָ.

Eternal God, open my lips, that my mouth may declare Your glory.

GOD OF ALL GENERATIONS   אבות ואמהות

בָּרוּךְ אַתָּה יי, אֱלֹהֵינוּ וֵאלֹהֵי אֲבוֹתֵינוּ וְאִמּוֹתֵינוּ:
אֱלֹהֵי אַבְרָהָם, אֱלֹהֵי יִצְחָק, וֵאלֹהֵי יַעֲקֹב.
אֱלֹהֵי שָׂרָה, אֱלֹהֵי רִבְקָה, אֱלֹהֵי לֵאָה, וֵאלֹהֵי רָחֵל.
הָאֵל הַגָּדוֹל הַגִּבּוֹר וְהַנּוֹרָא, אֵל עֶלְיוֹן, גּוֹמֵל חֲסָדִים
טוֹבִים וְקוֹנֵה הַכֹּל, וְזוֹכֵר חַסְדֵי אָבוֹת וְאִמָּהוֹת,
וּמֵבִיא גְאֻלָּה לִבְנֵי בְנֵיהֶם, לְמַעַן שְׁמוֹ בְּאַהֲבָה.
מֶלֶךְ עוֹזֵר וּמוֹשִׁיעַ וּמָגֵן.
בָּרוּךְ אַתָּה יי, מָגֵן אַבְרָהָם וְעֶזְרַת שָׂרָה.

Ba-ruch a-ta Adonai,
Eh-lo-hei-nu vei-lo-hei a-vo-tei-nu v'i-mo-tei-nu:
Eh-lo-hei Av-ra-ham, Eh-lo-hei Yitz-chak, vei-lo-hei Ya-a-kov.
Eh-lo-hei Sa-rah, Eh-lo-hei Riv-kah,
Eh-lo-hei Lei-ah, vei-lo-hei Ra-cheil.
Ha-eil ha-ga-dol ha-gi-bor v'ha-no-ra, Eil el-yon,
go-meil cha-sa-dim toh-vim, v'ko-nei ha-kol,
v'zo-cheir cha-s'dei a-voht v'i-ma-hoht,
u-mei-vi g'u-la li-v'nei v'nei-hem, l'ma-an sh'mo, b'a-ha-va.
Meh-lech o-zeir u-mo-shi-a u-ma-gein.
Ba-ruch a-ta Adonai, ma-gein Av-ra-ham v'ez-rat Sa-rah.

Praised be our God, the God of our fathers and our mothers:
God of Abraham, God of Isaac, and God of Jacob;
God of Sarah, God of Rebekah,
God of Leah and God of Rachel;
great, mighty, and awesome God, God supreme.
Ruler of all the living, Your ways are ways of love.
You remember the faithfulness of our ancestors,
and in love bring redemption to their children's children
for the sake of Your name.
You are our Sovereign and our Help,
our Redeemer and our Shield.
We praise You, O God, Shield of Abraham, Protector of Sarah.

GOD'S POWER גבורות

אַתָּה גִבּוֹר לְעוֹלָם, אֲדֹנָי, מְחַיֵּה הַכֹּל אַתָּה, רַב לְהוֹשִׁיעַ.
מְכַלְכֵּל חַיִּים בְּחֶסֶד, מְחַיֵּה הַכֹּל בְּרַחֲמִים רַבִּים.
סוֹמֵךְ נוֹפְלִים, וְרוֹפֵא חוֹלִים, וּמַתִּיר אֲסוּרִים,
וּמְקַיֵּם אֱמוּנָתוֹ לִישֵׁנֵי עָפָר. מִי כָמְוֹךָ בַּעַל גְּבוּרוֹת,
וּמִי דְּוֹמֶה לָּךְ, מֶלֶךְ מֵמִית וּמְחַיֶּה וּמַצְמִיחַ יְשׁוּעָה?
וְנֶאֱמָן אַתָּה לְהַחֲיוֹת הַכֹּל. בָּרוּךְ אַתָּה יי, מְחַיֵּה הַכֹּל.

A-ta gi-bor l'o-lam, Adonai, m'cha-yei ha-kol a-ta, rav l'ho-shi-a.
M'chal-keil cha-yim b'cheh-sed,
m'cha-yei ha-kol b'ra-cha-mim ra-bim.
So-meich no-f'lim, v'ro-fei cho-lim, u-ma-tir a-su-rim,
u-m'ka-yeim eh-mu-na-toh li-shei-nei a-far.
Mi cha-mo-cha ba-al g'vu-roht, u-mi doh-meh lach,
meh-lech mei-meet u-m'cha-yeh u-matz-mi-ach y'shu-a?
V'neh-eh-man a-ta l'ha-cha-yoht ha-kol.
Ba-ruch a-ta Adonai, m'cha-yei ha-kol.

Eternal is Your might, O God; all life is Your gift;
great is Your power to save!

⌣

22

With love You sustain the living,
with great compassion give life to all.
You send help to the falling and healing to the sick;
You bring freedom to the captive
and keep faith with those who sleep in the dust.

Who is like You, Mighty One?
Who is Your equal, Author of life and death,
Source of salvation?

We praise You, Eternal God, Source of life.

❖ ❖

FOR AN EVENING SERVICE

THE HOLINESS OF GOD   קְדוּשַׁת הַשֵּׁם

אַתָּה קָדוֹשׁ וְשִׁמְךָ קָדוֹשׁ, וּקְדוֹשִׁים בְּכָל־יוֹם יְהַלְלוּךָ סֶּלָה.
בָּרוּךְ אַתָּה יי, הָאֵל הַקָּדוֹשׁ.

You are holy, Your name is holy,
and those who strive to be holy declare Your glory day by day.

We praise You, Eternal One, the holy God.

❖

FOR A MORNING SERVICE

SANCTIFICATION   קְדוּשָׁה

נְקַדֵּשׁ אֶת־שִׁמְךָ בָּעוֹלָם, כְּשֵׁם שֶׁמַּקְדִּישִׁים אוֹתוֹ בִּשְׁמֵי
מָרוֹם, כַּכָּתוּב עַל־יַד נְבִיאֶךָ: וְקָרָא זֶה אֶל־זֶה וְאָמַר:

We sanctify Your name on earth, even as all things, to the ends
of time and space, proclaim Your holiness, and in the words of
the prophet we say:

קָדוֹשׁ, קָדוֹשׁ, קָדוֹשׁ יהוה צְבָאוֹת,
מְלֹא כָל־הָאָרֶץ כְּבוֹדוֹ.

Ka-dosh, ka-dosh, ka-dosh Adonai tz'va-oht,
m'lo chol ha-a-retz k'vo-doh.

Holy, holy, holy is the Eternal One, God of the Hosts of Heaven!
The whole earth is ablaze with Your glory!

לְעֻמָּתָם בָּרוּךְ יֹאמֵרוּ:

All being recounts Your praise:

בָּרוּךְ כְּבוֹד־יהוה מִמְּקוֹמוֹ.

Ba-ruch k'vod Adonai mim-ko-mo.

Praised be the glory of God in heaven and earth.

וּבְדִבְרֵי קָדְשְׁךָ כָּתוּב לֵאמֹר:

And this is Your sacred word:

יִמְלֹךְ יהוה לְעוֹלָם, אֱלֹהַיִךְ צִיּוֹן, לְדֹר וָדֹר. הַלְלוּיָהּ!

Yim-loch Adonai l'o-lam, Eh-lo-ha-yich Tzi-yon,
l'dor va-dor. Ha-l'lu-yah!

The Eternal One shall reign for ever;
your God, O Zion, from generation to generation. Halleluyah!

לְדוֹר וָדוֹר נַגִּיד גָּדְלֶךָ וּלְנֵצַח נְצָחִים קְדֻשָּׁתְךָ נַקְדִּישׁ.
וְשִׁבְחֲךָ, אֱלֹהֵינוּ, מִפִּינוּ לֹא יָמוּשׁ לְעוֹלָם וָעֶד.
בָּרוּךְ אַתָּה יי, הָאֵל הַקָּדוֹשׁ.

To all generations we will make known Your greatness, and to all eternity proclaim Your holiness. Your praise, O God, shall never depart from our lips.

We praise You, Eternal One, the holy God.

❖ ❖

24

FOR EVENING AND MORNING SERVICES

*(The Intermediate Benedictions, through
page 29, may be recited silently or together.)*

WISDOM   בינה

אַתָּה חוֹנֵן לְאָדָם דַּעַת וּמְלַמֵּד לֶאֱנוֹשׁ בִּינָה. חָנֵּנוּ מֵאִתְּךָ
דֵּעָה, בִּינָה וְהַשְׂכֵּל. בָּרוּךְ אַתָּה יי, חוֹנֵן הַדָּעַת.

BY YOUR GRACE we have the power to gain knowledge and to
learn wisdom. Favor us with knowledge, wisdom, and insight,
for You are their Source.

We praise You, O God, gracious Giver of knowledge.

REPENTANCE   תשובה

הַשִׁיבֵנוּ אָבִינוּ לְתוֹרָתֶךָ, וְקָרְבֵנוּ מַלְכֵּנוּ לַעֲבוֹדָתֶךָ,
וְהַחֲזִירֵנוּ בִּתְשׁוּבָה שְׁלֵמָה לְפָנֶיךָ.
בָּרוּךְ אַתָּה יי, הָרוֹצֶה בִּתְשׁוּבָה.

HELP US, our Creator, to return to Your Teaching; draw us near,
our Sovereign, to Your service; and bring us back into Your
presence in perfect repentance.

We praise You, O God: You delight in repentance.

FORGIVENESS   סליחה

סְלַח־לָנוּ אָבִינוּ כִּי חָטָאנוּ, מְחַל־לָנוּ מַלְכֵּנוּ כִּי פָשָׁעְנוּ,
כִּי מוֹחֵל וְסוֹלֵחַ אָתָּה.
בָּרוּךְ אַתָּה יי, חַנּוּן הַמַּרְבֶּה לִסְלוֹחַ.

FORGIVE US, our Creator, when we sin; pardon us, our
Sovereign, when we transgress; for You are eager to forgive.

We praise You, O God: You are gracious and quick to forgive.

REDEMPTION   גאולה

רְאֵה בְעָנְיֵנוּ וְרִיבָה רִיבֵנוּ, וּגְאָלֵנוּ מְהֵרָה לְמַעַן שְׁמֶךָ,
כִּי גּוֹאֵל חָזָק אָתָּה. בָּרוּךְ אַתָּה יי, גּוֹאֵל יִשְׂרָאֵל.

LOOK UPON OUR AFFLICTION and help us in our need; O mighty
Redeemer, redeem us speedily for Your name's sake.

We praise You, O God, Redeemer of Israel.

HEALTH   רפואה

רְפָאֵנוּ יי וְנֵרָפֵא, הוֹשִׁיעֵנוּ וְנִוָּשֵׁעָה, וְהַעֲלֵה רְפוּאָה
שְׁלֵמָה לְכָל־מַכּוֹתֵינוּ. בָּרוּךְ אַתָּה יי, רוֹפֵא הַחוֹלִים.

COMPASSIONATE SOURCE OF HEALING, heal us, and we shall be
healed; save us, and we shall be saved; grant us a perfect healing for all our infirmities.

(A personal prayer for one who is ill may be added here.)

We praise You, O God, Healer of the sick.

ABUNDANCE   ברכת השנים

בָּרֵךְ עָלֵינוּ, יי אֱלֹהֵינוּ, אֶת־הַשָּׁנָה הַזֹּאת
וְאֶת־כָּל־מִינֵי תְבוּאָתָהּ לְטוֹבָה. וְתֵן בְּרָכָה עַל־פְּנֵי הָאֲדָמָה
וְשַׂבְּעֵנוּ מִטּוּבֶךָ. בָּרוּךְ אַתָּה יי, מְבָרֵךְ הַשָּׁנִים.

BLESS THIS YEAR for us, Eternal God: may its produce bring us
well-being. Bestow Your blessing on the earth that all Your children may share its abundance in peace.

We praise You, O God, for You bless earth's seasons from year
to year.

FREEDOM   חרות

תְּקַע בְּשׁוֹפָר גָּדוֹל לְחֵרוּתֵנוּ, וְשָׂא נֵס לִפְדּוֹת עֲשׁוּקֵינוּ,
וְקוֹל דְּרוֹר יִשָּׁמַע בְּאַרְבַּע כַּנְפוֹת הָאָרֶץ.
בָּרוּךְ אַתָּה יי, פּוֹדֶה עֲשׁוּקִים.

SOUND THE GREAT SHOFAR to proclaim freedom, raise high the banner of liberation for the oppressed, and let the song of liberty be heard in the four corners of the earth.

We praise You, O God, Redeemer of the oppressed.

JUSTICE   משפט

עַל שׁוֹפְטֵי אֶרֶץ שְׁפוֹךְ רוּחֶךָ, וְהַדְרִיכֵם בְּמִשְׁפְּטֵי צִדְקֶךָ,
וּמְלוֹךְ עָלֵינוּ אַתָּה לְבַדֶּךָ, בְּחֶסֶד וּבְרַחֲמִים.
בָּרוּךְ אַתָּה יי, מֶלֶךְ אוֹהֵב צְדָקָה וּמִשְׁפָּט.

BESTOW YOUR SPIRIT upon the rulers of all lands; guide them, that they may govern justly. Then shall love and compassion be enthroned among us.

We praise You, Eternal One,
the Sovereign God who loves righteousness and justice.

ON EVIL   על הרשעה

וְלָרִשְׁעָה אַל־תְּהִי תִקְוָה, וְהַתּוֹעִים אֵלֶיךָ יָשׁוּבוּ,
וּמַלְכוּת זָדוֹן מְהֵרָה תְשַׁבֵּר.
תַּקֵּן מַלְכוּתְךָ בְּתוֹכֵנוּ, בְּקָרוֹב בְּיָמֵינוּ לְעוֹלָם וָעֶד.
בָּרוּךְ אַתָּה יי, הַמַּשְׁבִּית רֶשַׁע מִן־הָאָרֶץ.

LET THE REIGN OF EVIL afflict us no more. May every errant heart find its way back to You. O help us to shatter the dominion of arrogance, to raise up a better world, where virtue will ennoble the life of Your children.

We praise You, O God,
whose will it is that evil vanish from the earth.

THE RIGHTEOUS   עַל הַצַּדִּיקִים

עַל־הַצַּדִּיקִים וְעַל־הַחֲסִידִים וְעַל גֵּרֵי הַצֶּדֶק וְעָלֵינוּ יֶהֱמוּ
רַחֲמֶיךָ, יי אֱלֹהֵינוּ, וְתֵן שָׂכָר טוֹב לְכָל הַבּוֹטְחִים בְּשִׁמְךָ
בֶּאֱמֶת, וְשִׂים חֶלְקֵנוּ עִמָּהֶם לְעוֹלָם.
בָּרוּךְ אַתָּה יי, מִשְׁעָן וּמִבְטָח לַצַּדִּיקִים.

FOR THE RIGHTEOUS AND FAITHFUL of all humankind, for all who
join themselves to our people, for all who put their trust in You,
and for all honest men and women, we ask Your favor, Eternal
God. Grant that we may always be numbered among them.

We praise You, O God, Staff and Support of the righteous.

JERUSALEM   בּוֹנֵה יְרוּשָׁלַיִם

שְׁכוֹן, יי אֱלֹהֵינוּ, בְּתוֹךְ יְרוּשָׁלַיִם עִירֶךָ, וִיהִי שָׁלוֹם
בִּשְׁעָרֶיהָ, וְשַׁלְוָה בְּלֵב יוֹשְׁבֶיהָ, וְתוֹרָתְךָ מִצִּיּוֹן תֵּצֵא,
וּדְבָרְךָ מִירוּשָׁלָיִם. בָּרוּךְ אַתָּה יי, בּוֹנֵה יְרוּשָׁלָיִם.

LET YOUR PRESENCE be manifest in Jerusalem, Your city.
Establish peace in her gates and quietness in the hearts of all
who dwell there. Let Your Torah go forth from Zion, Your word
from Jerusalem.

We praise You, O God, Builder of Jerusalem.

DELIVERANCE   יְשׁוּעָה

אֶת־צֶמַח צְדָקָה מְהֵרָה תַצְמִיחַ, וְקֶרֶן יְשׁוּעָה תָרוּם
כִּנְאֻמֶךָ, כִּי לִישׁוּעָתְךָ קִוִּינוּ כָּל־הַיּוֹם.
בָּרוּךְ אַתָּה יי, מַצְמִיחַ קֶרֶן יְשׁוּעָה.

LET THE PLANT OF RIGHTEOUSNESS blossom and flourish, and let
the light of deliverance shine forth according to Your word, for
we await Your deliverance all the day.

We praise You, O God, who will cause the light of deliverance
to dawn for all the world.

28

PRAYER   שומע תפלה

שְׁמַע קוֹלֵנוּ, יי אֱלֹהֵינוּ, חוּס וְרַחֵם עָלֵינוּ, וּתְקַבֵּל
בְּרַחֲמִים וּבְרָצוֹן אֶת־תְּפִלָּתֵנוּ, כִּי אֵל שׁוֹמֵעַ תְּפִלּוֹת
וְתַחֲנוּנִים אָתָּה. בָּרוּךְ אַתָּה יי, שׁוֹמֵעַ תְּפִלָּה.

HEAR OUR VOICE, ETERNAL GOD; have compassion upon us, and accept our prayer with favor and mercy, for You are a God who hears prayer and supplication.

We praise You, O God: You hearken to prayer.

(The Intermediate Blessings end here)

All are seated

WORSHIP   עבודה

רְצֵה, יי אֱלֹהֵינוּ, בְּעַמְּךָ יִשְׂרָאֵל, וּתְפִלָּתָם בְּאַהֲבָה
תְקַבֵּל, וּתְהִי לְרָצוֹן תָּמִיד עֲבוֹדַת יִשְׂרָאֵל עַמֶּךָ.
אֵל קָרוֹב לְכָל־קֹרְאָיו, פְּנֵה אֶל עֲבָדֶיךָ וְחָנֵּנוּ;
שְׁפוֹךְ רוּחֲךָ עָלֵינוּ, וְתֶחֱזֶינָה עֵינֵינוּ בְּשׁוּבְךָ לְצִיּוֹן בְּרַחֲמִים.

בָּרוּךְ אַתָּה יי, הַמַּחֲזִיר שְׁכִינָתוֹ לְצִיּוֹן.

Be gracious, Eternal God, to Your people Israel, and receive our prayers with love. O may our worship always be acceptable to You.

Fill us with the knowledge that You are near to all who seek You in truth. Let our eyes behold Your presence in our midst and in the midst of our people in Zion. We praise You, O God, whose presence gives life to Zion and all Israel.

ON ROSH CHODESH

אֱלֹהֵינוּ וֵאלֹהֵי אֲבוֹתֵינוּ וְאִמּוֹתֵינוּ, יַעֲלֶה וְיָבֹא וְיִזָּכֵר
זִכְרוֹנֵנוּ וְזִכְרוֹן כָּל־עַמְּךָ בֵּית יִשְׂרָאֵל לְפָנֶיךָ לְטוֹבָה
לְחֵן לְחֶסֶד וּלְרַחֲמִים, לְחַיִּים וּלְשָׁלוֹם בְּיוֹם רֹאשׁ
הַחֹדֶשׁ הַזֶּה.

זָכְרֵנוּ, יְיָ אֱלֹהֵינוּ, בּוֹ לְטוֹבָה. אָמֵן.

וּפָקְדֵנוּ בוֹ לִבְרָכָה. אָמֵן.

וְהוֹשִׁיעֵנוּ בוֹ לְחַיִּים. אָמֵן.

Our God, God of our fathers and our mothers, be mindful of
Your people Israel on this first day of the new month,
and renew in us love and compassion, goodness, life, and peace.
This day remember us for well-being. *Amen.*
This day bless us with Your nearness. *Amen.*
This day help us to lead a full life. *Amen.*

❖ ❖

THANKSGIVING   הוֹדָאָה

מוֹדִים אֲנַחְנוּ לָךְ, שָׁאַתָּה הוּא יְיָ אֱלֹהֵינוּ וֵאלֹהֵי
אֲבוֹתֵינוּ וְאִמּוֹתֵינוּ לְעוֹלָם וָעֶד. צוּר חַיֵּינוּ, מָגֵן יִשְׁעֵנוּ,
אַתָּה הוּא לְדוֹר וָדוֹר. נוֹדֶה לְּךָ וּנְסַפֵּר תְּהִלָּתֶךָ, עַל־
חַיֵּינוּ הַמְּסוּרִים בְּיָדֶךָ, וְעַל־נִשְׁמוֹתֵינוּ הַפְּקוּדוֹת לָךְ,
וְעַל־נִסֶּיךָ שֶׁבְּכָל־יוֹם עִמָּנוּ, וְעַל־נִפְלְאוֹתֶיךָ וְטוֹבוֹתֶיךָ
שֶׁבְּכָל־עֵת, עֶרֶב וָבֹקֶר וְצָהֳרָיִם. הַטּוֹב: כִּי לֹא־כָלוּ
רַחֲמֶיךָ, וְהַמְרַחֵם: כִּי־לֹא תַמּוּ חֲסָדֶיךָ, מֵעוֹלָם קִוִּינוּ
לָךְ. וְעַל כֻּלָּם יִתְבָּרַךְ וְיִתְרוֹמַם שִׁמְךָ, מַלְכֵּנוּ, תָּמִיד
לְעוֹלָם וָעֶד.

וְכֹל הַחַיִּים יוֹדוּךָ סֶלָה, וִיהַלְלוּ אֶת שִׁמְךָ בֶּאֱמֶת,
הָאֵל יְשׁוּעָתֵנוּ וְעֶזְרָתֵנוּ סֶלָה.

בָּרוּךְ אַתָּה יְיָ, הַטּוֹב שִׁמְךָ וּלְךָ נָאֶה לְהוֹדוֹת.

30

We gratefully acknowledge that You are our God and the God of our people, the God of all the generations. You are the Rock of our life, the Power that shields us in every age. We thank You and sing Your praises: for our lives, which are in Your hand; for our souls, which are in Your keeping; for the signs of Your presence we encounter every day; and for Your wondrous gifts at all times, morning, noon, and night. You are Goodness: Your mercies never end; You are Compassion: Your love will never fail. You have always been our hope.

For all these things, O Sovereign God, let Your name be for ever exalted and blessed.

O God our Redeemer and Helper, let all who live affirm You and praise Your name in truth. Eternal God, whose nature is Goodness, we give You thanks and praise.

PEACE   ברכת שלום

FOR AN EVENING SERVICE

שָׁלוֹם רָב עַל־יִשְׂרָאֵל עַמְּךְ תָּשִׂים לְעוֹלָם,
כִּי אַתָּה הוּא מֶלֶךְ אָדוֹן לְכָל הַשָּׁלוֹם.
וְטוֹב בְּעֵינֶיךְ לְבָרֵךְ אֶת־עַמְּךְ יִשְׂרָאֵל
בְּכָל־עֵת וּבְכָל־שָׁעָה בִּשְׁלוֹמֶךְ.
בָּרוּךְ אַתָּה יי, הַמְבָרֵךְ אֶת־עַמּוֹ יִשְׂרָאֵל בַּשָּׁלוֹם.

Sha-lom rav al Yis-ra-eil am-cha ta-sim l'-o-lam,
ki a-ta hu meh-lech a-don l'chol ha-sha-lom,
v'tov b'ei-ne-cha l'va-reich et am-cha Yis-ra-eil
b'chol eit u-v'chol sha-ah bi-sh'lo-me-cha.
Ba-ruch a-ta Adonai ha-m'va-reich et a-mo Yis-ra-eil ba-sha-lom.

31

O Sovereign Source of peace,
let Israel Your people know enduring peace,
for it is good in Your sight to bless Israel continually
with Your peace.

We praise You, O God: You bless Israel with peace.

FOR A MORNING SERVICE

שִׂים שָׁלוֹם, טוֹבָה וּבְרָכָה, חֵן וָחֶסֶד וְרַחֲמִים,
עָלֵינוּ וְעַל־כָּל־יִשְׂרָאֵל עַמֶּךָ.
בָּרְכֵנוּ אָבִינוּ, כֻּלָּנוּ כְּאֶחָד, בְּאוֹר פָּנֶיךָ,
כִּי בְאוֹר פָּנֶיךָ נָתַתָּ לָנוּ, יְיָ אֱלֹהֵינוּ,
תּוֹרַת חַיִּים, וְאַהֲבַת חֶסֶד,
וּצְדָקָה וּבְרָכָה וְרַחֲמִים, וְחַיִּים וְשָׁלוֹם.
וְטוֹב בְּעֵינֶיךָ לְבָרֵךְ אֶת־עַמְּךָ יִשְׂרָאֵל
בְּכָל־עֵת וּבְכָל־שָׁעָה בִּשְׁלוֹמֶךָ.
בָּרוּךְ אַתָּה יְיָ, הַמְבָרֵךְ אֶת־עַמּוֹ יִשְׂרָאֵל בַּשָּׁלוֹם.

Sim sha-lom
to-vah uv'ra-cha chein va-che-sed v'ra-cha-mim
a-lei-nu v'al kol Yis-ra-eil, a-me-cha.

Ba-r'chei-nu a-vi-nu ku-la-nu k'e-chad b'or pa-ne-cha
ki b'or pa-ne-cha na-ta-ta la-nu Adonai Eh-lo-hei-nu.
To-rat cha-yim v'a-ha-vat che-sed
u-tz'da-ka u-v'ra-chah v'ra-cha-mim v'cha-yim v'sha-lom.

V'tov b'ei-neh-cha l'va-reich et a-m'cha Yis-ra-eil
b'chol eit u-v'chol sha-ah bi-sh'lo-me-cha.
Ba-ruch a-ta Adonai,
ha-m'va-reich et a-mo Yis-ra-eil ba-sha-lom.

Grant us peace, Your most precious gift,
O Eternal Source of peace,
and give us the will to proclaim its message
to all the peoples of the earth.

32

*Bless our country, that it may always be a stronghold of peace,
and its advocate among the nations.*

*May contentment reign within its borders,
health and happiness within its homes.*

*Strengthen the bonds of friendship
among the inhabitants of all lands,
and may the love of Your name hallow
every home and every heart.*

We praise You O God, the Source of peace.

❖ ❖

TO 85

SILENT PRAYER

אֱלֹהַי, נְצֹר לְשׁוֹנִי מֵרָע, וּשְׂפָתַי מִדַּבֵּר מִרְמָה. וְלִמְקַלְלַי נַפְשִׁי תִדּוֹם וְנַפְשִׁי כֶּעָפָר לַכֹּל תִּהְיֶה. פְּתַח לִבִּי בְּתוֹרָתֶךָ, וּבְמִצְוֹתֶיךָ תִּרְדֹּף נַפְשִׁי. וְכָל־הַחוֹשְׁבִים עָלַי רָעָה, מְהֵרָה הָפֵר עֲצָתָם וְקַלְקֵל מַחֲשַׁבְתָּם. עֲשֵׂה לְמַעַן שְׁמֶךָ, עֲשֵׂה לְמַעַן יְמִינֶךָ, עֲשֵׂה לְמַעַן קְדֻשָׁתֶךָ, עֲשֵׂה לְמַעַן תּוֹרָתֶךָ; לְמַעַן יֵחָלְצוּן יְדִידֶיךָ, הוֹשִׁיעָה יְמִינְךָ וַעֲנֵנִי.

O God, keep my tongue from evil and my lips from deceit. Help me to be silent in the face of derision, humble in the presence of all. Open my heart to Your Torah, and I will hasten to do Your Mitzvot. Save me with Your power; in time of trouble be my answer, that those who love You may rejoice.

❖ ❖

יִהְיוּ לְרָצוֹן אִמְרֵי־פִי וְהֶגְיוֹן לִבִּי לְפָנֶיךָ, יהוה, צוּרִי וְגֹאֲלִי.

Yi-h'yu l'ra-tson i-m'rei fi v'heg-yon li-bi l'fa-ne-cha,
Adonai tsu-ri v'go-a-li.

May the words of my mouth, and the meditations of my heart, be acceptable to You, O God, my Rock and my Redeemer.

❖

עֹשֶׂה שָׁלוֹם בִּמְרוֹמָיו, הוּא יַעֲשֶׂה שָׁלוֹם עָלֵינוּ וְעַל־כָּל־יִשְׂרָאֵל, וְאִמְרוּ אָמֵן.

O-seh sha-lom bi-m'ro-mav, hu ya-a-seh sha-lom
a-lei-nu v'al kol Yis-ra-eil, v'i-m'ru: A-mein.

May the One who causes peace to reign in the high heavens let peace descend on us, on all Israel, and all the world.

The Torah Service begins on page 79
Aleinu is on page 85

34

Welcoming Shabbat

SHALOM ALEICHEM   שלום עליכם

שָׁלוֹם עֲלֵיכֶם, מַלְאֲכֵי הַשָּׁרֵת, מַלְאֲכֵי עֶלְיוֹן,
מִמֶּלֶךְ מַלְכֵי הַמְּלָכִים, הַקָּדוֹשׁ בָּרוּךְ הוּא.

בּוֹאֲכֶם לְשָׁלוֹם, מַלְאֲכֵי הַשָּׁלוֹם, מַלְאֲכֵי עֶלְיוֹן,
מִמֶּלֶךְ מַלְכֵי הַמְּלָכִים, הַקָּדוֹשׁ בָּרוּךְ הוּא.

בָּרְכוּנִי לְשָׁלוֹם, מַלְאֲכֵי הַשָּׁלוֹם, מַלְאֲכֵי עֶלְיוֹן,
מִמֶּלֶךְ מַלְכֵי הַמְּלָכִים, הַקָּדוֹשׁ בָּרוּךְ הוּא.

צֵאתְכֶם לְשָׁלוֹם, מַלְאֲכֵי הַשָּׁלוֹם, מַלְאֲכֵי עֶלְיוֹן,
מִמֶּלֶךְ מַלְכֵי הַמְּלָכִים, הַקָּדוֹשׁ בָּרוּךְ הוּא.

Sha-lom a-lei-chem mal-a-chei ha-sha-reit, mal-a-chei el-yon,
Mi-me-lech ma-l'chei ham-la-chim, ha-ka-dosh ba-ruch hu.

Bo-a-chem l'sha-lom, mal-a-chei ha-sha-lom, mal-a-chei el-yon,
Mi-me-lech ma-l'chei ham-la-chim, ha-ka-dosh ba-ruch hu.

Bar'chu-ni l'sha-lom, mal-a-chei ha-sha-lom, mal-a-chei el-yon,
Mi-me-lech ma-l'chei ham-la-chim, ha-ka-dosh ba-ruch hu.

Tzei-t'chem l'sha-lom, mal-a-chei ha-sha-lom, mal-a-chei el-yon,
Mi-me-lech ma-l'chei ham-la-chim, ha-ka-dosh ba-ruch hu.

Peace be to you, O ministering angels, messengers of the Most High,
of the supreme Sovereign, the Holy One, ever to be praised.

Enter in peace, O messengers of the Most High, of the supreme Sovereign,
the Holy One, ever to be praised.

Bless us with peace, O messengers of the Most High,
of the supreme Sovereign, the Holy One, ever to be praised.

Depart in peace, O messengers of the Most High,
of the supreme Sovereign, the Holy One, ever to be praised.

WELCOMING SHABBAT

CANDLE LIGHTING   הדלקת הנרות

בָּרוּךְ אַתָּה יי, אֱלֹהֵינוּ מֶלֶךְ הָעוֹלָם, אֲשֶׁר קִדְּשָׁנוּ בְּמִצְוֹתָיו
וְצִוָּנוּ לְהַדְלִיק נֵר שֶׁל שַׁבָּת.

Ba-ruch a-ta Adonai, Eh-lo-hei-nu meh-lech ha-o-lam
ah-sher ki-d'sha-nu b'mitz-vo-tav v'tzi-va-nu
l'had-lik ner shel Shabbat.

We praise You, Eternal God, Sovereign of the universe: You call
us to holiness, and enjoin us to kindle the Sabbath lights.

May we be blessed with Sabbath joy.

May we be blessed with Sabbath peace.

May we be blessed with Sabbath light.

KIDDUSH   קדוש

Raise the Kiddush cups filled with wine or grape juice

בָּרוּךְ אַתָּה יי, אֱלֹהֵינוּ מֶלֶךְ הָעוֹלָם, בּוֹרֵא פְּרִי הַגָּפֶן.

בָּרוּךְ אַתָּה יי, אֱלֹהֵינוּ מֶלֶךְ הָעוֹלָם, אֲשֶׁר קִדְּשָׁנוּ
בְּמִצְוֹתָיו וְרָצָה בָנוּ, וְשַׁבַּת קָדְשׁוֹ בְּאַהֲבָה וּבְרָצוֹן
הִנְחִילָנוּ זִכָּרוֹן לְמַעֲשֵׂה בְרֵאשִׁית. כִּי הוּא יוֹם תְּחִלָּה
לְמִקְרָאֵי קֹדֶשׁ, זֵכֶר לִיצִיאַת מִצְרָיִם. כִּי־בָנוּ בָחַרְתָּ
וְאוֹתָנוּ קִדַּשְׁתָּ מִכָּל־הָעַמִּים, וְשַׁבַּת קָדְשְׁךָ בְּאַהֲבָה
וּבְרָצוֹן הִנְחַלְתָּנוּ. בָּרוּךְ אַתָּה יי, מְקַדֵּשׁ הַשַּׁבָּת.

Ba-ruch a-ta Adonai, Eh-lo-hei-nu meh-lech ha-o-lam,
bo-rei p'ri ha-ga-fen.

Ba-ruch a-ta Adonai, Eh-lo-hei-nu meh-lech ha-o-lam,
a-sher ki-d'sha-nu b'mitz-vo-tav v'ra-tza va-nu,
v'sha-bat kod-sho b'a-ha-va u-v'ra-tzon hin-chi-la-nu,
zi-ka-ron l'ma-a-sei v'rei-sheet.
Ki hu yom t'chi-la l'mik-ra-ei ko-desh, zei-cher li-tzi-at Mitz-ra-yim.

36

Ki va-nu va-char-ta v'o-ta-nu ki-dash-ta mi-kol ha-a-mim,

v'sha-bat kod-sh'cha b'a-ha-va u-v'ra-tzon hin-chal-ta-nu.

Ba-ruch a-ta Adonai, m'ka-deish ha-sha-bat.

We praise You, Eternal God, Sovereign of the universe:
You create the fruit of the vine.

We praise You, Eternal God, Sovereign of the universe:
You call us to holiness with the Mitzvah of Shabbat:
the sign of Your love, a reminder of Your creative work,
and of our liberation from Egyptian bondage: our day of days.
On Shabbat especially, we hearken to Your call
to serve You as a holy people.

We praise You, O God, for the holiness of Shabbat.

Drink

MOTZI   מוֹצִיא

בָּרוּךְ אַתָּה יי, אֱלֹהֵינוּ מֶלֶךְ הָעוֹלָם,
הַמוֹצִיא לֶחֶם מִן הָאָרֶץ.

Ba-ruch a-ta Adonai, Eh-lo-hei-nu meh-lech ha-o-lam,

ha-mo-tzi le-chem min ha-a-retz.

We praise You, Eternal God, Sovereign of the universe:
You cause bread to come forth from the earth.

Slice or tear the challah and distribute it around the table to be eaten.
Dinner is served.

Blessings After the Meal   ברכת המזון

A PILGRIM SONG   שיר המעלות

שִׁיר הַמַּעֲלוֹת, בְּשׁוּב יהוה אֶת־שִׁיבַת צִיּוֹן, הָיִינוּ כְּחֹלְמִים.
אָז יִמָּלֵא שְׂחוֹק פִּינוּ, וּלְשׁוֹנֵנוּ רִנָּה. אָז יֹאמְרוּ בַגּוֹיִם:
הִגְדִּיל יהוה לַעֲשׂוֹת עִם־אֵלֶּה. הִגְדִּיל יהוה לַעֲשׂוֹת עִמָּנוּ,
הָיִינוּ שְׂמֵחִים! שׁוּבָה יהוה אֶת־שְׁבִיתֵנוּ כַּאֲפִיקִים בַּנֶּגֶב.
הַזֹּרְעִים בְּדִמְעָה בְּרִנָּה יִקְצֹרוּ. הָלוֹךְ יֵלֵךְ וּבָכֹה, נֹשֵׂא
מֶשֶׁךְ־הַזָּרַע, בֹּא־יָבוֹא בְרִנָּה נֹשֵׂא אֲלֻמֹּתָיו.

Shir ha-ma-a-lot, b'-shuv Adonai
et shi-vat tzi-yon ha-yi-nu k'chol-mim.
Az yi-ma-lei s'chok pi-nu ul'sho-nei-nu ri-na.
Az yom-ru va-go-yim hig-dil Adonai la-a-sot im ei-leh.
Hig-dil Adonai la-a-sot i-ma-nu, ha-yi-nu s'mei-chim!
Shu-vah Adonai et sh'vi-tei-nu ka-a-fi-kim ba-ne-gev.
Ha-zo-rim b'di-mah b'ri-nah yik-tzo-ru.
Ha-loch yei-lech u-va-cho no-sei meh-shech ha-za-rah,
bo ya-vo v'ri-nah no-sei a-lu-mo-tav.

When God restores the exiles to Zion, it will seem like a dream. Our mouths will fill with laughter, our tongues with joyful song. They will say among the nations: "God has done great things for them." Yes, God is doing great things for us, and we are joyful. Restore our fortunes, O God, as streams revive the desert. Then those who have sown in tears shall reap in joy. Those who go forth weeping, carrying bags of seeds, shall come home with shouts of joy, bearing their sheaves.

❖ ❖

BLESSINGS AFTER THE MEAL

ON WEEKDAYS BEGIN HERE.

Leader:

חֲבֵרִים וַחֲבֵרוֹת, נְבָרֵךְ.

Cha-vei-rim v'cha-vei-rot n'va-reich.

Let us praise God.

Group:

יְהִי שֵׁם יי מְבֹרָךְ מֵעַתָּה וְעַד עוֹלָם.

Y'hi sheim Adonai m'vo-rach mei-a-ta v'ad o-lam!

Praised be the name of God, now and for ever!

Leader:

יְהִי שֵׁם יי מְבֹרָךְ מֵעַתָּה וְעַד עוֹלָם.
בִּרְשׁוּת הַחֲבְרָה, נְבָרֵךְ אֱלֹהֵינוּ שֶׁאָכַלְנוּ מִשֶּׁלוֹ.

Y'hi sheim Adonai m'vo-rach mei-a-ta v'ad o-lam!
Bir-shut ha-chev-rah, n'va-reich E-lo-hei-nu she-a-chal-nu mi-she-lo.

Praised be the name of God, now and for ever!
Praised be our God, of whose abundance we have eaten.

Group:

בָּרוּךְ אֱלֹהֵינוּ שֶׁאָכַלְנוּ מִשֶּׁלוֹ, וּבְטוּבוֹ חָיִינוּ.

Ba-ruch E-lo-hei-nu she-a-chal-nu mi-she-lo, uv-tu-vo cha-yi-nu.

Praised be our God,
of whose abundance we have eaten, and by whose goodness we live.

Leader:

בָּרוּךְ אֱלֹהֵינוּ שֶׁאָכַלְנוּ מִשֶּׁלוֹ, וּבְטוּבוֹ חָיִינוּ.
בָּרוּךְ הוּא וּבָרוּךְ שְׁמוֹ.

Ba-ruch E-lo-hei-nu she-a-chal-nu mi-she-lo, uv-tu-vo cha-yi-nu.
Ba-ruch hu u–va-ruch sh'mo.

Praised be our God,
of whose abundance we have eaten, and by whose goodness we live.
Praised be the Eternal God!

❖ ❖

BLESSINGS AFTER THE MEAL

Group:

בָּרוּךְ אַתָּה יי, אֱלֹהֵינוּ מֶלֶךְ הָעוֹלָם,

הַזָּן אֶת־הָעוֹלָם כֻּלּוֹ בְּטוּבוֹ, בְּחֵן בְּחֶסֶד וּבְרַחֲמִים.

הוּא נוֹתֵן לֶחֶם לְכָל־בָּשָׂר, כִּי לְעוֹלָם חַסְדּוֹ.

וּבְטוּבוֹ הַגָּדוֹל תָּמִיד לֹא חָסַר לָנוּ, וְאַל יֶחְסַר לָנוּ,

מָזוֹן לְעוֹלָם וָעֶד, בַּעֲבוּר שְׁמוֹ הַגָּדוֹל.

כִּי הוּא אֵל זָן וּמְפַרְנֵס לַכֹּל,

וּמֵטִיב לַכֹּל וּמֵכִין מָזוֹן לְכָל־בְּרִיּוֹתָיו אֲשֶׁר בָּרָא.

בָּרוּךְ אַתָּה יי, הַזָּן אֶת־הַכֹּל.

Ba-ruch a-ta Adonai, E-lo-hei-nu me-lech ha-o-lam,

ha-zan et ha-o-lam ku-lo b'tu-vo, b'chein, b'che-sed, u-v'ra-cha-mim.

Hu no-tein le-chem l'chol ba-sar, ki l'o-lam chas-do.

U-v'tu-vo ha-ga-dol ta-mid lo cha-sar la-nu,

v'al yech-sar la-nu ma-zon l'o-lam va-ed, ba-a-vur sh'mo ha-ga-dol.

Ki hu Eil zan u-m'far-neis la-kol u-mei-tiv la-kol

u-mei-chin ma-zon l'chol b'ri-yo-tav a-sher ba-ra.

Ba-ruch a-ta Adonai, ha-zan et ha-kol.

Sovereign God of the universe, we praise You: Your goodness sustains the world. You are the God of grace, love, and compassion, the Source of bread for all who live—for Your love is everlasting. Through Your great goodness we never lack for food; You provide food enough for all. We praise You, Source of food for all who live. Amen.

כַּכָּתוּב: וְאָכַלְתָּ וְשָׂבָעְתָּ, וּבֵרַכְתָּ אֶת־יהוה אֱלֹהֶיךָ

עַל־הָאָרֶץ הַטֹּבָה אֲשֶׁר נָתַן־לָךְ.

בָּרוּךְ אַתָּה יי, עַל־הָאָרֶץ וְעַל־הַמָּזוֹן.

Ka-ka-tuv: V'a-chal-ta v'sa-va-ta, u-vei-rach-ta

et Adonai E-lo-he-cha

al ha-a-retz ha-to-vah a-sher na-tan lach.

Ba-ruch a-ta A-do-nai, al ha-a-rets v'al ha-ma-zon.

As it is written in the Torah: You shall eat, be satisfied and bless the Eternal One your God for the good land given to you.

We praise You, O God, for the earth and for sustenance.

וּבְנֵה יְרוּשָׁלַיִם עִיר הַקֹּדֶשׁ בִּמְהֵרָה בְיָמֵינוּ.

בָּרוּךְ אַתָּה יי, בּוֹנֶה בְּרַחֲמָיו יְרוּשָׁלַיִם. אָמֵן.

U-v'nei Y'ru-sha-la-yim ir ha-ko-desh bi-m'hei-ra b'ya-mei-nu.

Ba-ruch a-ta Adonai, bo-neh b'ra-cha-mav Y'ru-sha-la-yim, A-mein.

Let Jerusalem, the holy city, be renewed in our time.
We praise You, who in compassion rebuild Jerusalem. Amen.

❖ ❖

ON SHABBAT

הָרַחֲמָן, הוּא יַנְחִילֵנוּ יוֹם שֶׁכֻּלוֹ שַׁבָּת.

וּמְנוּחָה לְחַיֵּי הָעוֹלָמִים.

Ha-ra-cha-man, hu yan-chi-lei-nu yom she-ku-lo sha-bat.

U-me-nu-cha le-cha-yei ha-o-la-mim.

Merciful One, help us to see the coming of a time that is all Shabbat.

❖ ❖

עֹשֶׂה שָׁלוֹם בִּמְרוֹמָיו, הוּא יַעֲשֶׂה שָׁלוֹם

עָלֵינוּ וְעַל־כָּל־יִשְׂרָאֵל, וְאִמְרוּ אָמֵן.

O-seh sha-lom bi-m'ro-mav, hu ya-a-seh sha-lom

a-lei-nu v'al kol Yis-ra-eil, v'i-m'ru, A-mein.

May the Source of perfect peace grant peace to us, to all Israel,
and to all the world.

יהוה עֹז לְעַמּוֹ יִתֵּן, יהוה יְבָרֵךְ אֶת־עַמּוֹ בַשָּׁלוֹם.

Adonai oz l'a-mo yi-tein, Adonai y'va-reich et a-mo va-sha-lom.

Eternal God: give strength to Your people;
Eternal God: bless Your people with peace.

Shabbat Evening Service ערבית לשבת

לְכָה דוֹדִי לִקְרַאת כַּלָּה, פְּנֵי שַׁבָּת נְקַבְּלָה.
לְכָה דוֹדִי לִקְרַאת כַּלָּה, פְּנֵי שַׁבָּת נְקַבְּלָה.

L'cha do-di lik-rat ka-la, p'nei sha-bat n'ka-b'la.
L'cha do-di lik-rat ka-la, p'nei sha-bat n'ka-b'la.

"שָׁמוֹר" וְ"זָכוֹר", בְּדִבּוּר אֶחָד, הִשְׁמִיעָנוּ אֵל הַמְיֻחָד.
יי אֶחָד וּשְׁמוֹ אֶחָד, לְשֵׁם וּלְתִפְאֶרֶת וְלִתְהִלָּה.

לְכָה דוֹדִי. . .

Sha-mor v'za-chor b'di-bur e-chad, hish-mi-a-nu Eil ha-m'yu-chad.
Adonai e-chad u-sh'mo e-chad, l'sheim u-l'tif-e-ret v'li-t'hi-la.

Le-cha do-di. . .

הִתְעוֹרְרִי, הִתְעוֹרְרִי, כִּי בָא אוֹרֵךְ! קוּמִי, אוֹרִי,
עוּרִי עוּרִי, שִׁיר דַּבֵּרִי; כְּבוֹד יי עָלַיִךְ נִגְלָה.

לְכָה דוֹדִי. . .

Hit-o-r'ri, hit-o-r'ri, ki va o-reich! Ku-mi, o-ri,
u-ri u-ri, shir da-bei-ri; k'vod Adonai a-la-yich nig-la.

Le-cha do-di. . .

בּוֹאִי בְשָׁלוֹם, עֲטֶרֶת בַּעְלָהּ, גַּם בְּשִׂמְחָה וּבְצָהֳלָה,
תּוֹךְ אֱמוּנֵי עַם סְגֻלָּה, בּוֹאִי כַלָּה! בּוֹאִי כַלָּה!

לְכָה דוֹדִי. . .

Bo-i v'sha-lom, a-te-ret ba-a-la; gam b'sim-cha u-v'tso-ho-la,
toch e-mu-nei am s'gu-la. Bo-i cha-la! Bo-i cha-la!

Le-cha do-di. . .

Beloved, come to meet the bride; beloved, come to greet Shabbat.

Keep and remember: a single command, the Only God caused us to hear;
the Eternal is One, God's name is One, for honor and glory and praise.

Awake, awake, your light has come! Arise, shine, awake and sing;
the Eternal's glory dawns upon you.

Enter in peace, O crown of your husband; enter in gladness, enter in joy.
Come to the people that keeps its faith. Enter, O bride! Enter, O bride!

❖ ❖

O Source of light and truth,
Creator of the eternal law of goodness,
and of the impulse within us for justice and mercy,
we pray that this hour of worship may be
one of vision and inspiration.
Help us to find knowledge by which to live;
lead us to take the words we shall speak
into our hearts and our lives.

Bless all who enter this sanctuary in search and in need,
all who bring to this place the offering of their hearts.
May our worship here lead us to fulfill our words and our hopes
with acts of kindness, peace, and love. Amen.

❖ ❖

We have come together to strengthen our bonds with our people
Israel. Like Jews of generations past, we celebrate the grandeur
of creation. Like Jews of every age, we echo our people's
ancient call for justice.

Our celebration is a sharing of memory and hope.

We are Jews, but each of us is unique. We stand apart and alone,
with differing feelings and insights. And yet we are not entirely
alone and separate, for we are children of one people and one
heritage.

Our celebration unites many separate selves
into a single chorus.

And we are one in search of life's meaning. All of us know despair and exaltation; all bear burdens; all have moments of weakness and times of strength; all sing songs of sorrow and love.

May our celebration bring us strength along our way.

In this circle of hope, in the presence of the sacred, may the heart come to know itself and its best, finding a fresh impulse to love the good.

May our celebration lead us to work for the good; and may this Shabbat give strength to us and to our people Israel.

❖ ❖

הִנֵּה מַה־טּוֹב וּמַה נָּעִים
שֶׁבֶת אַחִים גַּם יָחַד.

Hi-nei mah tov u-mah na-im sheh-vet a-chim gam ya-chad.

Behold how good and how pleasant for people to dwell together in unity.

❖ ❖

Many are the generations of Israel, and in every age we have sought the living God through Sabbath rest and worship. This time and place hold the power to increase our joy in the Eternal. O God, even as we seek You in the sanctuary, help us to know that Your glory fills all space; make us understand that You are with us at all times, if we but open our minds to You.

We feel the presence of Your spirit in our homes and on our ways; we see the beauty of Your creation in mountain, sea, and sky, and in the human form; we hear You in the silence of our own hearts speaking the truths the heart knows.

May we be Your witness to the world,
Your messenger to all the earth.

*May we show forth Your image within us,
the divine spark that makes us human.*

❖ ❖

All rise

READER'S KADDISH   חצי קדיש

יִתְגַּדַּל וְיִתְקַדַּשׁ שְׁמֵהּ רַבָּא בְּעָלְמָא דִי־בְרָא כִרְעוּתֵהּ,
וְיַמְלִיךְ מַלְכוּתֵהּ בְּחַיֵּיכוֹן וּבְיוֹמֵיכוֹן וּבְחַיֵּי דְכָל־בֵּית
יִשְׂרָאֵל, בַּעֲגָלָא וּבִזְמַן קָרִיב, וְאִמְרוּ: אָמֵן.

יְהֵא שְׁמֵהּ רַבָּא מְבָרַךְ לְעָלַם וּלְעָלְמֵי עָלְמַיָּא.

יִתְבָּרַךְ וְיִשְׁתַּבַּח, וְיִתְפָּאַר וְיִתְרוֹמַם וְיִתְנַשֵּׂא, וְיִתְהַדָּר
וְיִתְעַלֶּה וְיִתְהַלַּל שְׁמֵהּ דְּקֻדְשָׁא, בְּרִיךְ הוּא, לְעֵלָּא
מִן־כָּל־בִּרְכָתָא וְשִׁירָתָא, תֻּשְׁבְּחָתָא וְנֶחֱמָתָא
דַּאֲמִירָן בְּעָלְמָא, וְאִמְרוּ: אָמֵן.

Yit-ga-dal v'yit-ka-dash sh'mei ra-ba b'al-ma di-v'ra chir-u-tei,
v'yam-lich mal-chu-tei b'cha-yei-chon u-v'yo-mei-chon u-v'cha-yei
d'chol beit Yis-ra-eil, ba-a-ga-la u-viz-man ka-riv, v'i-m'ru: A-mein.

Y'hei sh'mei ra-ba m'va-rach l'a-lam u-l'al-mei al-ma-ya.

Yit-ba-rach v'yish-ta-bach v'yit-pa-ar, v'yit-ro-mam, v'yit-na-sei,
v'yit-ha-dar, v'yit-a-leh, v'yit-ha-lal sh'mei d'kud-sha, b'rich hu,
l'ei-la min kol bir-cha-ta v'shi-ra-ta, tush-b'cha-ta v'neh-cheh-ma-ta
da-a-mi-ran b'al-ma, v'i-m'ru: A-mein.

The Sh'ma and Its Blessings   שמע וברכותיה

בָּרְכוּ אֶת־יי הַמְבֹרָךְ!

Praise the One to whom our praise is due!

בָּרוּךְ יי הַמְבֹרָךְ לְעוֹלָם וָעֶד!

Ba-ruch Adonai ha-m'vo-rach l'o-lam va-ed!

Praised be the One to whom our praise is due, now and for ever!

CREATION   מעריב ערבים

בָּרוּךְ אַתָּה יי, אֱלֹהֵינוּ מֶלֶךְ הָעוֹלָם,
אֲשֶׁר בִּדְבָרוֹ מַעֲרִיב עֲרָבִים, בְּחָכְמָה פּוֹתֵחַ שְׁעָרִים,
וּבִתְבוּנָה מְשַׁנֶּה עִתִּים, וּמַחֲלִיף אֶת־הַזְּמַנִּים,
וּמְסַדֵּר אֶת־הַכּוֹכָבִים בְּמִשְׁמְרוֹתֵיהֶם בָּרָקִיעַ כִּרְצוֹנוֹ.

בּוֹרֵא יוֹם וָלָיְלָה, גּוֹלֵל אוֹר מִפְּנֵי חֹשֶׁךְ וְחֹשֶׁךְ מִפְּנֵי אוֹר,
וּמַעֲבִיר יוֹם וּמֵבִיא לָיְלָה, וּמַבְדִּיל בֵּין יוֹם וּבֵין לָיְלָה,
יי צְבָאוֹת שְׁמוֹ. אֵל חַי וְקַיָּם, תָּמִיד יִמְלוֹךְ עָלֵינוּ
לְעוֹלָם וָעֶד. בָּרוּךְ אַתָּה יי, הַמַּעֲרִיב עֲרָבִים.

As day departs, as the dark of night descends, we lift our eyes to the heavens. In awe and wonder our hearts cry out:

Eternal God, how majestic is Your name in all the earth!

A vast universe: who can know it? We look out to the endless suns and ask: What are we? What are our dreams and our hopes? What are we, that You are mindful of us? What are we, that You should care for us?

And yet within us abides a measure of Your spirit. You are remote, but, oh, how near! Ordering the stars in the vast solitudes of the dark, yet whispering in the mind that You are closer than the air we breathe. With love and awe we turn to You, and in the dark of evening seek the light of Your presence. For You have made us little less than Divine, and crowned us with glory and honor!

REVELATION   אהבת עולם

אַהֲבַת עוֹלָם בֵּית יִשְׂרָאֵל עַמְּךָ אָהֶבְתָּ.

תּוֹרָה וּמִצְוֹת, חֻקִּים וּמִשְׁפָּטִים אוֹתָנוּ לִמַּדְתָּ.

עַל־כֵּן, יי אֱלֹהֵינוּ, בְּשָׁכְבֵנוּ וּבְקוּמֵנוּ נָשִׂיחַ בְּחֻקֶּיךָ,
וְנִשְׂמַח בְּדִבְרֵי תוֹרָתֶךָ וּבְמִצְוֹתֶיךָ לְעוֹלָם וָעֶד.

כִּי הֵם חַיֵּינוּ וְאֹרֶךְ יָמֵינוּ, וּבָהֶם נֶהְגֶּה יוֹמָם וָלָיְלָה.
וְאַהֲבָתְךָ אַל־תָּסוּר מִמֶּנּוּ לְעוֹלָמִים!
בָּרוּךְ אַתָּה יי, אוֹהֵב עַמּוֹ יִשְׂרָאֵל.

One and Only God, You have make each of us unique, and formed us to be united in one family of life. Be with us, Eternal One, as we seek to unite our lives with Your power and Your love.

We proclaim now Your Oneness and our own hope for unity; we acclaim Your creative power in the universe and in ourselves, the Law that binds world to world and heart to heart:

❖ ❖

שְׁמַע יִשְׂרָאֵל: יהוה אֱלֹהֵינוּ, יהוה אֶחָד!

Sh'ma Yis-ra-eil: Adonai Eh-lo-hei-nu, Adonai Eh-chad!

Hear, O Israel: the Eternal One is our God,
the Eternal God alone!

בָּרוּךְ שֵׁם כְּבוֹד מַלְכוּתוֹ לְעוֹלָם וָעֶד!

Ba-ruch sheim k'vod mal-chu-toh l'o-lam va-ed!

Blessed is God's glorious majesty for ever and ever!

All are seated

וְאָהַבְתָּ אֵת יְהֹוָה אֱלֹהֶיךָ בְּכָל־לְבָבְךָ וּבְכָל־נַפְשְׁךָ
וּבְכָל־מְאֹדֶךָ: וְהָיוּ הַדְּבָרִים הָאֵלֶּה אֲשֶׁר אָנֹכִי מְצַוְּךָ
הַיּוֹם עַל־לְבָבֶךָ: וְשִׁנַּנְתָּם לְבָנֶיךָ וְדִבַּרְתָּ בָּם בְּשִׁבְתְּךָ
בְּבֵיתֶךָ וּבְלֶכְתְּךָ בַדֶּרֶךְ וּבְשָׁכְבְּךָ וּבְקוּמֶךָ: וּקְשַׁרְתָּם
לְאוֹת עַל־יָדֶךָ וְהָיוּ לְטֹטָפֹת בֵּין עֵינֶיךָ: וּכְתַבְתָּם
עַל־מְזוּזֹת בֵּיתֶךָ וּבִשְׁעָרֶיךָ:

לְמַעַן תִּזְכְּרוּ וַעֲשִׂיתֶם אֶת־כָּל־מִצְוֹתָי וִהְיִיתֶם קְדֹשִׁים
לֵאלֹהֵיכֶם: אֲנִי יְהֹוָה אֱלֹהֵיכֶם אֲשֶׁר הוֹצֵאתִי אֶתְכֶם
מֵאֶרֶץ מִצְרַיִם לִהְיוֹת לָכֶם לֵאלֹהִים. אֲנִי יְהֹוָה אֱלֹהֵיכֶם:

V'a-hav-ta et Adonai Eh-lo-heh-cha
b'chol l'va-v'cha u-v'chol naf-sh'cha u-v'chol m'o-deh-cha.
V'ha-yu ha-d'va-rim ha-ei-leh
a-sher a-no-chi m'tza-v'cha ha-yom al l'va-veh-cha.
V'shi-nan-tam l'va-neh-cha v'di-bar-ta bam
b'shiv-t'cha b'vei-teh-cha u-v'lech-t'cha va-deh-rech
u-v'shoch-b'cha u-v'ku-meh-cha. U-k'shar-tam l'oht al ya-deh-cha
v'ha-yu l'toh-ta-foht bein ei-neh-cha;
uch'tav-tam al m'zu-zoht bei-teh-cha u-vish'a-reh-cha.

L'ma-an tiz-k'ru va-a-si-tem et kol mitz-vo-tai,
vi-h'yi-tem k'doh-shim lei-lo-hei-chem.
A-ni Adonai Eh-lo-hei-chem
a-sher ho-tzei-ti et-chem mei-eh-retz mitz-ra-yim
li-h'yoht la-chem lei-lo-him.
A-ni Adonai Eh-lo-hei-chem.

You shall love the Eternal One, your God, with all your heart, with all your mind, with all your being. Set these words, which I command you this day, upon your heart. Teach them faithfully to your children; speak of them in your home and on your way, when you lie down and when you rise up. Bind them as a sign upon your hand; let them be a symbol before your eyes; inscribe them on the doorposts of your house, and on your gates.

Be mindful of all My Mitzvot, and do them:
so shall you consecrate yourselves to your God.
I am your Eternal God who led you out of Egypt to be your
God; I am your Eternal God.

REDEMPTION   גאולה

In a world torn by violence and pain, a world far from
wholeness and peace, a world waiting still to be redeemed, give
us, O Source of good, the courage to say: There is one God in
heaven and earth.

The high heavens declare Your glory; may earth reveal Your
justice and Your love.

From Egypt, the house of bondage, we were delivered; at Sinai,
amid peals of thunder, we bound ourselves to Your purpose.
Inspired by prophets and instructed by sages, we survived
oppression and exile, time and again overcoming the forces that
would have destroyed us.

Our failings are many — are faults are great — yet it has been our
glory to bear witness to our God, and to keep alive in dark ages
the vision of a world redeemed.

May this vision never fade; let us continue to work for the day
when the nations will be one and at peace. Then shall we sing
with one accord, as Moses, Miriam, and Israel sang at the shores
of the Sea:

מִי־כָמְֹכָה בָּאֵלִם, יהוה?
מִי כָּמְכָה, נֶאְדָּר בַּקֹּדֶשׁ,
נוֹרָא תְהִלֹּת, עְׂשֵׂה פֶלֶא?

מַלְכוּתְךָ רָאוּ בָנֶיךָ, בּוֹקֵעַ יָם לִפְנֵי מֹשֶׁה; זֶה אֵלִי!
עָנוּ וְאָמְרוּ: יהוה יִמְלֹךְ לְעֹלָם וָעֶד!

וְנֶאֱמַר: כִּי פָדָה יי אֶת־יַעֲקֹב, וּגְאָלוֹ מִיַּד חָזָק מִמֶּנּוּ.
בָּרוּךְ אַתָּה יי, גָּאַל יִשְׂרָאֵל.

49

Mi cha-mo-cha ba-ei-lim, Adonai?
Mi ka-mo-cha, neh-dar ba-ko-desh,
no-ra t'hi-loht, o-sei feh-leh?

Mal-chu-t'cha ra-u va-neh-cha, bo-kei-a yam lif-nei Mo-sheh;
zeh Ei-li! A-nu v'a-m'ru: Adonai yim-loch l'o-lam va-ed.

V'neh-eh-mar: Ki fa-da Adonai et Ya-a-kov,
u-g'a-lo mi-yad cha-zak mi-meh-nu.
Ba-ruch a-ta Adonai, ga-al Yis-ra-eil.

Who is like You, Eternal One, among the gods that are worshipped? Who is like You, majestic in holiness, awesome in splendor, doing wonders?

In their escape from the sea, Your children saw Your sovereign might displayed. "This is my God!" they cried. "The Eternal will reign for ever and ever!"

And it has been said: The Eternal One delivered Jacob, and redeemed us from the hand of one stronger than ourselves. We praise You, Eternal One, Redeemer of Israel.

DIVINE PROVIDENCE הַשְׁכִּיבֵנוּ

הַשְׁכִּיבֵנוּ, יי אֱלֹהֵינוּ, לְשָׁלוֹם, וְהַעֲמִידֵנוּ, מַלְכֵּנוּ, לַחַיִּים.
וּפְרוֹשׂ עָלֵינוּ סֻכַּת שְׁלוֹמֶךָ, וְתַקְּנֵנוּ בְּעֵצָה טוֹבָה מִלְּפָנֶיךָ,
וְהוֹשִׁיעֵנוּ לְמַעַן שְׁמֶךָ, וְהָגֵן בַּעֲדֵנוּ. וְהָסֵר מֵעָלֵינוּ אוֹיֵב,
דֶּבֶר וְחֶרֶב וְרָעָב וְיָגוֹן; וְהָסֵר שָׂטָן מִלְּפָנֵינוּ וּמֵאַחֲרֵינוּ,
וּבְצֵל כְּנָפֶיךָ תַּסְתִּירֵנוּ, כִּי אֵל שׁוֹמְרֵנוּ וּמַצִּילֵנוּ אָתָּה,
כִּי אֵל מֶלֶךְ חַנּוּן וְרַחוּם אָתָּה. וּשְׁמוֹר צֵאתֵנוּ וּבוֹאֵנוּ
לְחַיִּים וּלְשָׁלוֹם, מֵעַתָּה וְעַד עוֹלָם.
בָּרוּךְ אַתָּה יי, פּוֹרֵשׂ סֻכַּת שָׁלוֹם עָלֵינוּ,
וְעַל־כָּל־עַמּוֹ־יִשְׂרָאֵל, וְעַל יְרוּשָׁלָיִם.

Let there be love and understanding among us; let peace and friendship be our shelter from life's storms. Eternal God, help us to walk with good companions, to live with hope in our hearts and eternity in our thoughts, that we may lie down in peace and rise up to find our hearts waiting to do Your will.

We praise You, Guardian of Israel, whose love gives light to all the world.

❖ ❖

O God of Israel, may our worship on this day help us to grow in loyalty to our covenant with You and to the way of life it demands: the way of gentleness and justice, the path of truth and of peace.

THE COVENANT OF SHABBAT   ושמרו

וְשָׁמְרוּ בְנֵי־יִשְׂרָאֵל אֶת־הַשַּׁבָּת,

לַעֲשׂוֹת אֶת־הַשַּׁבָּת לְדֹרֹתָם בְּרִית עוֹלָם.

בֵּינִי וּבֵין בְּנֵי יִשְׂרָאֵל אוֹת הִיא לְעֹלָם

כִּי שֵׁשֶׁת יָמִים עָשָׂה יְיָ אֶת־הַשָּׁמַיִם וְאֶת־הָאָרֶץ,

וּבַיּוֹם הַשְּׁבִיעִי שָׁבַת וַיִּנָּפַשׁ.

V'sha-m'ru v'nei Yis-ra-eil et ha-sha-bat,
la-a-sot et ha-sha-bat l'do-ro-tam b'rit o-lam.
Bei-ni u-vein b'nei Yis-ra-eil ot hi l'o-lam.
Ki shei-shet ya-mim a-sa Adonai et ha-sha-ma-yim v'et ha-a-rets,
u-va-yom ha-sh'vi-i, sha-vat va-yi-na-fash.

The people of Israel shall keep the Sabbath, observing the Sabbath in every generation as a covenant for all time. It is a sign for ever between Me and the people of Israel, for in six days the Eternal God made heaven and earth, taking rest and refreshment on the seventh day.

MEDITATION

Prayer invites God's Presence to suffuse our spirits, God's will to prevail in our lives. Prayer cannot bring water to parched fields, nor mend a broken bridge, nor rebuild a ruined city; but prayer can water an arid soul, mend a broken heart, and rebuild a weakened will.

51

T'filah תפלה

All rise

אֲדֹנָי, שְׂפָתַי תִּפְתָּח וּפִי יַגִּיד תְּהִלָּתֶךָ.

Eternal God, open my lips, that my mouth may declare Your glory.

GOD OF ALL GENERATIONS   אבות ואמהות

בָּרוּךְ אַתָּה יי, אֱלֹהֵינוּ וֵאלֹהֵי אֲבוֹתֵינוּ וְאִמּוֹתֵינוּ:
אֱלֹהֵי אַבְרָהָם, אֱלֹהֵי יִצְחָק, וֵאלֹהֵי יַעֲקֹב.
אֱלֹהֵי שָׂרָה, אֱלֹהֵי רִבְקָה, אֱלֹהֵי לֵאָה, וֵאלֹהֵי רָחֵל.
הָאֵל הַגָּדוֹל הַגִּבּוֹר וְהַנּוֹרָא, אֵל עֶלְיוֹן, גּוֹמֵל חֲסָדִים
טוֹבִים וְקוֹנֵה הַכֹּל, וְזוֹכֵר חַסְדֵי אָבוֹת וְאִמָּהוֹת,
וּמֵבִיא גְאֻלָּה לִבְנֵי בְנֵיהֶם, לְמַעַן שְׁמוֹ בְּאַהֲבָה.
מֶלֶךְ עוֹזֵר וּמוֹשִׁיעַ וּמָגֵן.
בָּרוּךְ אַתָּה יי, מָגֵן אַבְרָהָם וְעֶזְרַת שָׂרָה.

Ba-ruch a-ta Adonai,
Eh-lo-hei-nu vei-lo-hei a-vo-tei-nu v'i-mo-tei-nu:
Eh-lo-hei Av-ra-ham, Eh-lo-hei Yitz-chak, vei-lo-hei Ya-a-kov.
Eh-lo-hei Sa-rah, Eh-lo-hei Riv-kah,
Eh-lo-hei Lei-ah, vei-lo-hei Ra-cheil.
Ha-eil ha-ga-dol ha-gi-bor, v'ha-no-ra, Eil el-yon,
go-meil cha-sa-dim toh-vim, v'ko-nei ha-kol,
v'zo-cheir chas-dei a-vot v'i-ma-hoht,
u-mei-vi g'u-la li-v'nei v'nei-hem, l'ma-an sh'mo, b'a-ha-va.
Meh-lech o-zeir u-mo-shi-a u-ma-gein.
Ba-ruch a-ta Adonai, ma-gein Av-ra-ham v'ez-rat Sa-rah.

Praised be our God, the God of our fathers and our mothers:
God of Abraham, God of Isaac, and God of Jacob;
God of Sarah, God of Rebekah,
God of Leah and God of Rachel;
great, mighty, and awesome God, God supreme.
Ruler of all the living, Your ways are ways of love.
You remember the faithfulness of our ancestors,

and in love bring redemption to their children's children
for the sake of Your name.
You are our Sovereign and our Help,
our Redeemer and our Shield.
We praise You, O God, Shield of Abraham, Protector of Sarah.

GOD'S POWER   גבורות

אַתָּה גִבּוֹר לְעוֹלָם, אֲדֹנָי, מְחַיֵּה הַכֹּל אַתָּה, רַב לְהוֹשִׁיעַ.
מְכַלְכֵּל חַיִּים בְּחֶסֶד, מְחַיֵּה הַכֹּל בְּרַחֲמִים רַבִּים.
סוֹמֵךְ נוֹפְלִים, וְרוֹפֵא חוֹלִים, וּמַתִּיר אֲסוּרִים,
וּמְקַיֵּם אֱמוּנָתוֹ לִישֵׁנֵי עָפָר. מִי כָמוֹךָ בַּעַל גְּבוּרוֹת,
וּמִי דוֹמֶה לָּךְ, מֶלֶךְ מֵמִית וּמְחַיֶּה וּמַצְמִיחַ יְשׁוּעָה?
וְנֶאֱמָן אַתָּה לְהַחֲיוֹת הַכֹּל. בָּרוּךְ אַתָּה יי, מְחַיֵּה הַכֹּל.

A-ta gi-bor l'o-lam, Adonai, m'cha-yei ha-kol a-ta, rav l'ho-shi-a.
M'chal-keil cha-yim b'cheh-sed,
m'cha-yei ha-kol b'ra-cha-mim ra-bim.
So-meich no-f'lim, v'ro-fei cho-lim, u-ma-tir a-su-rim,
u-m'ka-yeim eh-mu-na-toh li-shei-nei a-far.
Mi cha-mo-cha ba-al g'vu-roht, u-mi doh-meh lach,
meh-lech mei-meet u-m'cha-yeh u-matz-mi-ach y'shu-a?
V'neh-eh-man a-ta l'ha-cha-yoht ha-kol.
Ba-ruch a-ta Adonai, m'cha-yei ha-kol.

Eternal is Your might, O God; all life is Your gift;
great is Your power to save!

With love You sustain the living,
with great compassion give life to all.
You send help to the falling and healing to the sick;
You bring freedom to the captive
and keep faith with those who sleep in the dust.

Who is like You, Mighty One?
Who is Your equal, Author of life and death,
Source of salvation?

We praise You, Eternal God, Source of life.

THE HOLINESS OF GOD   קדושת השם

אַתָּה קָדוֹשׁ וְשִׁמְךָ קָדוֹשׁ, וּקְדוֹשִׁים בְּכָל־יוֹם יְהַלְלוּךָ סֶּלָה.
בָּרוּךְ אַתָּה יי, הָאֵל הַקָּדוֹשׁ.

You are holy, Your name is holy,
and those who strive to be holy declare Your glory day by day.

We praise You, Eternal One, the holy God.

All are seated

THE HOLINESS OF SHABBAT   קדושת היום

אֱלֹהֵינוּ וֵאלֹהֵי אֲבוֹתֵינוּ וְאִמּוֹתֵינוּ, רְצֵה בִמְנוּחָתֵנוּ. קַדְּשֵׁנוּ
בְּמִצְוֹתֶיךָ וְתֵן חֶלְקֵנוּ בְּתוֹרָתֶךָ. שַׂבְּעֵנוּ מִטּוּבֶךָ, וְשַׂמְּחֵנוּ
בִּישׁוּעָתֶךָ, וְטַהֵר לִבֵּנוּ לְעָבְדְּךָ בֶּאֱמֶת. וְהַנְחִילֵנוּ, יי אֱלֹהֵינוּ,
בְּאַהֲבָה וּבְרָצוֹן שַׁבַּת קָדְשֶׁךָ, וְיָנוּחוּ בָה יִשְׂרָאֵל מְקַדְּשֵׁי
שְׁמֶךָ. בָּרוּךְ אַתָּה יי, מְקַדֵּשׁ הַשַּׁבָּת.

*God of Israel, may our worship on this Sabbath bring us near to
all that is high and holy. May it bind the generations in bonds of
love and sharing, and unite us with our people in common hope
and faith. And through Sabbath rest and worship, may we learn to
find fulfillment and joy in the vision of peace for all the world.*

WORSHIP   עבודה

רְצֵה, יי אֱלֹהֵינוּ, בְּעַמְּךָ יִשְׂרָאֵל, וּתְפִלָּתָם בְּאַהֲבָה תְקַבֵּל,
וּתְהִי לְרָצוֹן תָּמִיד עֲבוֹדַת יִשְׂרָאֵל עַמֶּךָ.
בָּרוּךְ אַתָּה יי, שֶׁאוֹתְךָ לְבַדְּךָ בְּיִרְאָה נַעֲבוֹד.

You are with us in our prayer, in our love and our doubt, in our
longing to feel Your presence and do Your will. You are the still,
clear voice within us. Therefore, O God, when doubt troubles

us, when anxiety makes us tremble, and pain clouds the mind, we look inward for the answer to our prayers. There may we find You, and there find courage, insight, and endurance. And let our worship bring us closer to one another, that all Israel, and all who seek You, may find new strength for Your service.

THANKSGIVING   הודאה

מוֹדִים אֲנַחְנוּ לָךְ, שָׁאַתָּה הוּא יי אֱלֹהֵינוּ וֵאלֹהֵי
אֲבוֹתֵינוּ וְאִמּוֹתֵינוּ לְעוֹלָם וָעֶד. צוּר חַיֵּינוּ, מָגֵן יִשְׁעֵנוּ,
אַתָּה הוּא לְדוֹר וָדוֹר. נוֹדֶה לְךָ וּנְסַפֵּר תְּהִלָּתֶךָ, עַל־
חַיֵּינוּ הַמְּסוּרִים בְּיָדֶךָ, וְעַל־נִשְׁמוֹתֵינוּ הַפְּקוּדוֹת לָךְ,
וְעַל־נִסֶּיךָ שֶׁבְּכָל־יוֹם עִמָּנוּ, וְעַל־נִפְלְאוֹתֶיךָ וְטוֹבוֹתֶיךָ
שֶׁבְּכָל־עֵת, עֶרֶב וָבֹקֶר וְצָהֳרָיִם. הַטּוֹב: כִּי לֹא־כָלוּ
רַחֲמֶיךָ, וְהַמְרַחֵם: כִּי־לֹא תַמּוּ חֲסָדֶיךָ, מֵעוֹלָם קִוִּינוּ
לָךְ. וְעַל כֻּלָּם יִתְבָּרַךְ וְיִתְרוֹמַם שִׁמְךָ, מַלְכֵּנוּ, תָּמִיד
לְעוֹלָם וָעֶד.
וְכֹל הַחַיִּים יוֹדוּךָ סֶּלָה, וִיהַלְלוּ אֶת שִׁמְךָ בֶּאֱמֶת,
הָאֵל יְשׁוּעָתֵנוּ וְעֶזְרָתֵנוּ סֶלָה.
בָּרוּךְ אַתָּה יי, הַטּוֹב שִׁמְךָ וּלְךָ נָאֶה לְהוֹדוֹת.

We gratefully acknowledge that You are our God and the God of our people, the God of all generations. You are the Rock of our life, the Power that shields us in every age. We thank You and sing Your praises: for our lives, which are in Your hand; for our souls, which are in Your keeping; for the signs of Your presence we encounter every day; and for Your wondrous gifts at all times, morning, noon and night. You are Goodness: Your mercies never end; You are Compassion: Your love will never fail. You have always been our hope.

For all these things, O Sovereign God, let Your name be for ever exalted and blessed.

PEACE

ברכת שלום

שָׁלוֹם רָב עַל־יִשְׂרָאֵל עַמְּךָ תָּשִׂים לְעוֹלָם,
כִּי אַתָּה הוּא מֶלֶךְ אָדוֹן לְכָל הַשָּׁלוֹם.
וְטוֹב בְּעֵינֶיךָ לְבָרֵךְ אֶת־עַמְּךָ יִשְׂרָאֵל
בְּכָל־עֵת וּבְכָל־שָׁעָה בִּשְׁלוֹמֶךָ.
בָּרוּךְ אַתָּה יי, הַמְבָרֵךְ אֶת־עַמּוֹ יִשְׂרָאֵל בַּשָּׁלוֹם.

Sha-lom rav al Yis-ra-eil a-m'cha ta-sim l'o-lam,
ki a-ta hu meh-lech a-don l'chol ha-sha-lom,
v'tov b'ei-ne-cha l'va-reich et a-m'cha Yis-ra-eil
b'chol eit u-v'chol sha-a bi-sh'lo-meh-cha.
Ba-ruch a-ta Adonai, ha-m'va-reich et a-mo Yis-ra-eil ba-sha-lom.

*Grant us peace, Your most precious gift, O Eternal Source of
peace, and give us the will to proclaim its message to all the
peoples of the earth. Bless our country, that it may always be a
stronghold of peace, and its advocate among the nations. May
contentment reign within its borders, health and happiness
within its homes. Strengthen the bonds of friendship among the
inhabitants of all lands, and may the love of Your name hallow
every home and every heart. We praise You, Eternal One, the
Source of peace.*

MEDITATION

These quiet moments of Shabbat open my soul. Blessed with
another week of life, I give thanks to the One who creates and
sustains me.

For all the good I have known during the days that have passed,
I am very grateful. I know that I have not always responded
with my best effort, but often I did earnestly try. I have tried to
give my family love and devotion, and I pray that I may grow
more loving as the years pass.

Even as I regret my weaknesses, I rejoice in my
accomplishments. Let these achievements, O God, lead to many
others. May I be blessed on each Shabbat with the sense of
having grown in goodness and compassion.

56

❖ ❖

יִהְיוּ לְרָצוֹן אִמְרֵי־פִי וְהֶגְיוֹן לִבִּי לְפָנֶיךָ, יהוה, צוּרִי וְגֹאֲלִי.

Yi-h'yu l'ra-tson i-m'rei fi v'-heg-yon li-bi l'fa-ne-cha,
Adonai tsu-ri v'go-a-li.

May the words of my mouth, and the meditations of my heart,
be acceptable to You, O God, my Rock and my Redeemer.

❖

עֹשֶׂה שָׁלוֹם בִּמְרוֹמָיו, הוּא יַעֲשֶׂה שָׁלוֹם
עָלֵינוּ וְעַל־כָּל־יִשְׂרָאֵל, וְאִמְרוּ אָמֵן.

O-seh sha-lom bim-ro-mav, hu ya-a-seh sha-lom
a-lei-nu v'al kol Yis-ra-eil, v'im-ru: A-mein.

May the One who causes peace to reign in the high heavens
let peace descend on us, on all Israel, and all the world.

Aleinu is on page 85

57

Shabbat Morning Service   שחרית לשבת

FOR THOSE WHO WEAR THE TALLIT

בָּרְכִי נַפְשִׁי אֶת יְיָ! יְיָ אֱלֹהַי, גָּדַלְתָּ מְּאֹד!
הוֹד וְהָדָר לָבָשְׁתָּ, עֹטֶה אוֹר כַּשַּׂלְמָה, נוֹטֶה שָׁמַיִם כַּיְרִיעָה.

Praise the Eternal One, O my soul!
O God, You are very great!
Arrayed in glory and majesty, You wrap Yourself in light as
with a garment, You stretch out the heavens like a curtain.

בָּרוּךְ אַתָּה יְיָ, אֱלֹהֵינוּ מֶלֶךְ הָעוֹלָם,
אֲשֶׁר קִדְּשָׁנוּ בְּמִצְוֹתָיו וְצִוָּנוּ לְהִתְעַטֵּף בַּצִּיצִת.

We praise You, Eternal God, Sovereign of the universe:
You hallow us with Your Mitzvot,
and teach us to wrap ourselves in the fringed Tallit.

58

MEDITATION

Each of us enters this sanctuary with a different need.

Some hearts are full of gratitude and joy:
They are overflowing with the happiness of love
and the joy of life;
they are eager to confront the day, to make the world more fair;
they are recovering from illness or have escaped misfortune.
And we rejoice with them.

Some hearts ache with sorrow:
Disappointments weigh heavily upon them,
and they have tasted despair;
families have been broken; loved ones lie on a bed of pain;
death has taken those whom they cherished.
May our presence and sympathy bring them comfort.

Some hearts are embittered:
They have sought answers in vain;
ideals are mocked and betrayed;
life has lost its meaning and value.
May the knowledge that we, too, are searching,
restore their hope and give them courage
to believe that not all is emptiness.

Some spirits hunger:
They long for friendship;
they crave understanding; they yearn for warmth.

May we in our common need and striving
gain strength from one another,
as we share our joys, lighten each other's burdens,
and pray for the welfare of our community.

FOR THE BLESSING OF WORSHIP   מה טבו

מַה־טֹבוּ אֹהָלֶיךָ, יַעֲקֹב, מִשְׁכְּנֹתֶיךָ, יִשְׂרָאֵל!

וַאֲנִי, בְּרֹב חַסְדְּךָ אָבֹא בֵיתֶךָ,

אֶשְׁתַּחֲוֶה אֶל־הֵיכַל קָדְשְׁךָ בְּיִרְאָתֶךָ.

יהוה, אָהַבְתִּי מְעוֹן בֵּיתֶךָ, וּמְקוֹם מִשְׁכַּן כְּבוֹדֶךָ.

וַאֲנִי אֶשְׁתַּחֲוֶה וְאֶכְרָעָה, אֶבְרְכָה לִפְנֵי־יהוה עֹשִׂי.

וַאֲנִי תְפִלָּתִי לְךָ, יהוה, עֵת רָצוֹן.

אֱלֹהִים בְּרָב־חַסְדֶּךָ, עֲנֵנִי בֶּאֱמֶת יִשְׁעֶךָ.

Mah to-vu o-ha-leh-cha Ya-a-kov, mish-k'no-teh-cha, Yis-ra-eil!

Va-a-ni, b'rov chas-d'cha a-vo vei-teh-cha,
esh-ta-cha-veh el hei-chal kod-sh'cha b'-yir-a-teh-cha.

Adonai a-hav-ti m'on bei-te-cha u-m'kom mish-kan k'vo-deh-cha.
Va-a-ni esh-ta-cha-veh v'ech-ra-ah, ev-r'chah li-f'nei Adonai o-si.

Va-a-ni t'fi-la-ti l'cha Adonai eit ra-tson.
Eh-lo-him b'rov chas-deh-cha a-nei-ni beh-eh-met yish-eh-cha.

How lovely are Your tents, O Jacob, your dwelling-places, O Israel!

As for me, O God abounding in grace,
I enter Your house to worship with awe in Your sacred place.

I love Your house, Eternal One, the dwelling-place of Your glory;
humbly I worship You, humbly I seek blessing from God my Maker.

To You, Eternal One, goes my prayer: may this be a time of Your
favor. In Your great love, O God, answer me with Your saving truth.

FOR HEALTH   אשר יצר

We praise You, Eternal God, Sovereign of the universe: With
Divine wisdom You have made our bodies, combining veins,
arteries, and vital organs into a finely balanced network.

Wondrous Maker and Sustainer of life, were one of them to fail
— how well we are aware! — we would lack the strength to
stand in life before You.

Source of our health and strength, we give You thanks and
praise.

FOR TORAH   לעסוק בדברי תורה

בָּרוּךְ אַתָּה יי, אֱלֹהֵינוּ מֶלֶךְ הָעוֹלָם, אֲשֶׁר קִדְּשָׁנוּ בְּמִצְוֹתָיו
וְצִוָּנוּ לַעֲסוֹק בְּדִבְרֵי תוֹרָה.

*We praise You, Eternal God, Sovereign of the universe: You hallow
us with the gift of Torah and invite us to immerse ourselves in its
words.*

*Eternal our God, make the words of Your Torah sweet to us, and to
the House of Israel, Your people, that we and our children may be
lovers of Your name and students of Your Torah. We praise You, O
God, Teacher of Torah to Your people Israel.*

אֵלּוּ דְבָרִים שֶׁאֵין לָהֶם שִׁעוּר, שֶׁאָדָם אוֹכֵל פֵּרוֹתֵיהֶם
בָּעוֹלָם הַזֶּה וְהַקֶּרֶן קַיֶּמֶת לוֹ לָעוֹלָם הַבָּא, וְאֵלּוּ הֵן:

These are obligations without measure, whose reward too, is
without measure:

To honor father and mother;	כִּבּוּד אָב וָאֵם,
to perform acts of love and kindness;	וּגְמִילוּת חֲסָדִים,
to attend the house of study daily;	וְהַשְׁכָּמַת בֵּית הַמִּדְרָשׁ שַׁחֲרִית וְעַרְבִית,
to welcome the stranger;	וְהַכְנָסַת אוֹרְחִים,
to visit the sick;	וּבִקּוּר חוֹלִים,
to rejoice with bride and groom;	וְהַכְנָסַת כַּלָּה,
to console the bereaved;	וּלְוָיַת הַמֵּת,

61

to pray with sincerity;

וְעִיּוּן תְּפִלָּה,

to make peace when there is strife.

וַהֲבָאַת שָׁלוֹם

בֵּין אָדָם לַחֲבֵרוֹ;

וְתַלְמוּד תּוֹרָה כְּנֶגֶד כֻּלָּם.

And the study of Torah leads to them all.

FOR THE SOUL   אלהי נשמה

אֱלֹהַי, נְשָׁמָה שֶׁנָּתַתָּ בִּי טְהוֹרָה הִיא! אַתָּה בְרָאתָהּ,

אַתָּה יְצַרְתָּהּ, אַתָּה נְפַחְתָּהּ בִּי, וְאַתָּה מְשַׁמְּרָהּ בְּקִרְבִּי.

כָּל־זְמַן שֶׁהַנְּשָׁמָה בְקִרְבִּי, מוֹדֶה אֲנִי לְפָנֶיךָ,

יי אֱלֹהַי וֵאלֹהֵי אֲבוֹתַי וְאִמּוֹתַי, רִבּוֹן כָּל־הַמַּעֲשִׂים,

אֲדוֹן כָּל־הַנְּשָׁמוֹת.

בָּרוּךְ אַתָּה יי, אֲשֶׁר בְּיָדוֹ נֶפֶשׁ כָּל־חָי, וְרוּחַ כָּל־בְּשַׂר־אִישׁ.

The soul that You have given me, O God, is pure! You created and formed it, breathed it into me, and within me You sustain it. So long as I have breath, therefore, I will give thanks to You, my God and God of all ages, Source of all being, loving Guide of every human spirit.

We praise You, O God, in whose hands are the souls of all the living and the spirits of all flesh.

FOR OUR BLESSINGS נסים בכל יום

בָּרוּךְ אַתָּה יי, אֱלֹהֵינוּ מֶלֶךְ הָעוֹלָם,
אֲשֶׁר נָתַן לַשֶּׂכְוִי בִינָה לְהַבְחִין בֵּין יוֹם וּבֵין לָיְלָה.

We praise You, Eternal God, Sovereign of the universe:
You have implanted mind and instinct within every living being.

בָּרוּךְ אַתָּה יי, אֱלֹהֵינוּ מֶלֶךְ הָעוֹלָם, שֶׁעָשַׂנִי יִשְׂרָאֵל.

Praised be the Eternal God, who has made me a Jew.

בָּרוּךְ אַתָּה יי, אֱלֹהֵינוּ מֶלֶךְ הָעוֹלָם, שֶׁעָשַׂנִי בֶּן חוֹרִין.

Praised be the Eternal God, who has made me to be free.

בָּרוּךְ אַתָּה יי, אֱלֹהֵינוּ מֶלֶךְ הָעוֹלָם, פּוֹקֵחַ עִוְרִים.

Praised be the Eternal God, who helps the blind to see.

בָּרוּךְ אַתָּה יי, אֱלֹהֵינוּ מֶלֶךְ הָעוֹלָם, מַלְבִּישׁ עֲרֻמִּים.

Praised be the Eternal God, who clothes the naked.

בָּרוּךְ אַתָּה יי, אֱלֹהֵינוּ מֶלֶךְ הָעוֹלָם, מַתִּיר אֲסוּרִים.

Praised be the Eternal God, who frees the captive.

בָּרוּךְ אַתָּה יי, אֱלֹהֵינוּ מֶלֶךְ הָעוֹלָם, זוֹקֵף כְּפוּפִים.

Praised be the Eternal God, who lifts up the fallen.

בָּרוּךְ אַתָּה יי, אֱלֹהֵינוּ מֶלֶךְ הָעוֹלָם, הַמֵּכִין מִצְעֲדֵי־גָבֶר.

Praised be the Eternal God, who makes firm our steps.

בָּרוּךְ אַתָּה יי, אֱלֹהֵינוּ מֶלֶךְ הָעוֹלָם, אוֹזֵר יִשְׂרָאֵל בִּגְבוּרָה.

Praised be the Eternal God,
who girds our people Israel with strength.

בָּרוּךְ אַתָּה יי, אֱלֹהֵינוּ מֶלֶךְ הָעוֹלָם,
עוֹטֵר יִשְׂרָאֵל בְּתִפְאָרָה.

Praised be the Eternal God, who crowns Israel with glory.

63

בָּרוּךְ אַתָּה יי, אֱלֹהֵינוּ מֶלֶךְ הָעוֹלָם, הַנּוֹתֵן לַיָּעֵף כֹּחַ.

Praised be the Eternal God, who gives strength to the weary.

בָּרוּךְ אַתָּה יי, אֱלֹהֵינוּ מֶלֶךְ הָעוֹלָם,
הַמַּעֲבִיר שֵׁנָה מֵעֵינַי וּתְנוּמָה מֵעַפְעַפָּי.

Praised be the Eternal God,
who removes sleep from the eyes, slumber from the eyelids.

FOR CONSCIENCE   תורה ומצוות

Eternal One, our God and God of all ages, school us in Your
Torah and bind us to Your Mitzvot.

Help us to keep far from sin, to master temptation, and to avoid
falling under its spell. May our darker passions not rule us, nor
evil companions lead us astray.

Strengthen in us the voice of conscience; prompt us to deeds of
goodness; and bend our every impulse to Your service, so that
this day and always we may know Your love and the good will
of all who behold us. We praise You, O God: You bestow love
and kindness on Your people Israel.

❖ ❖

At all times let us revere God inwardly as well as outwardly,
acknowledge the truth and speak it in our hearts.

All rise

READER'S KADDISH   חצי קדיש

יִתְגַּדַּל וְיִתְקַדַּשׁ שְׁמֵהּ רַבָּא בְּעָלְמָא דִי־בְרָא כִרְעוּתֵהּ,
וְיַמְלִיךְ מַלְכוּתֵהּ בְּחַיֵּיכוֹן וּבְיוֹמֵיכוֹן וּבְחַיֵּי דְכָל־בֵּית
יִשְׂרָאֵל, בַּעֲגָלָא וּבִזְמַן קָרִיב, וְאִמְרוּ: אָמֵן.

יְהֵא שְׁמֵהּ רַבָּא מְבָרַךְ לְעָלַם וּלְעָלְמֵי עָלְמַיָּא.

יִתְבָּרַךְ וְיִשְׁתַּבַּח, וְיִתְפָּאַר וְיִתְרוֹמַם וְיִתְנַשֵּׂא, וְיִתְהַדָּר
וְיִתְעַלֶּה וְיִתְהַלָּל שְׁמֵהּ דְּקוּדְשָׁא, בְּרִיךְ הוּא, לְעֵלָּא
מִן־כָּל־בִּרְכָתָא וְשִׁירָתָא, תֻּשְׁבְּחָתָא וְנֶחֱמָתָא
דַּאֲמִירָן בְּעָלְמָא, וְאִמְרוּ: אָמֵן.

Yit-ga-dal v'yit-ka-dash sh'mei ra-ba b'al-ma di-v'ra chir-u-tei,
v'yam-lich mal-chu-tei b'cha-yei-chon u-v'yo-mei-chon u-v'cha-yei
d'chol beit Yis-ra-eil, ba-a-ga-la u-viz-man ka-riv, v'i-m'ru: A-mein.

Y'hei sh'mei ra-ba m'va-rach l'a-lam u-l'al-mei al-ma-ya.

Yit-ba-rach v'yish-ta-bach v'yit-pa-ar, v'yit-ro-mam, v'yit-na-sei,
v'yit-ha-dar, v'yit-a-leh, v'yit-ha-lal sh'mei d'kud-sha, b'rich hu,
l'ei-la min kol bir-cha-ta v'shi-ra-ta, tush-b'cha-ta v'neh-cheh-ma-ta
da-a-mi-ran b'al-ma, v'i-m'ru: A-mein.

The Sh'ma and Its Blessings שמע וברכותיה

בָּרְכוּ אֶת־יי הַמְבֹרָךְ!

Praise the One to whom our praise is due!

בָּרוּךְ יי הַמְבֹרָךְ לְעוֹלָם וָעֶד!

Ba-ruch Adonai ha-m'vo-rach l'o-lam va-ed!

Praised be the One to whom our praise is due, now and for ever!

CREATION   יוצר

בָּרוּךְ אַתָּה יי, אֱלֹהֵינוּ מֶלֶךְ הָעוֹלָם, יוֹצֵר אוֹר וּבוֹרֵא
חֹשֶׁךְ, עֹשֶׂה שָׁלוֹם וּבוֹרֵא אֶת־הַכֹּל. הַמֵּאִיר לָאָרֶץ
וְלַדָּרִים עָלֶיהָ בְּרַחֲמִים, וּבְטוּבוֹ מְחַדֵּשׁ בְּכָל־יוֹם תָּמִיד
מַעֲשֵׂה בְרֵאשִׁית. מָה רַבּוּ מַעֲשֶׂיךָ, יי! כֻּלָּם בְּחָכְמָה עָשִׂיתָ,
מָלְאָה הָאָרֶץ קִנְיָנֶךָ. תִּתְבָּרַךְ, יי אֱלֹהֵינוּ, עַל־שֶׁבַח מַעֲשֵׂה
יָדֶיךָ, וְעַל־מְאוֹרֵי־אוֹר שֶׁעָשִׂיתָ: יְפָאֲרוּךָ. סֶּלָה.
בָּרוּךְ אַתָּה יי, יוֹצֵר הַמְּאוֹרוֹת.

We praise You, Eternal God, Sovereign of the universe, whose mercy makes light to shine over the earth and all its inhabitants, and whose goodness renews day by day the work of creation.

How manifold are Your works, O God! In wisdom You have made them all. The heavens declare Your glory. The earth reveals Your creative power. You form light and darkness, bring harmony into nature, and peace to the human heart.

We praise You, O God, Creator of light.

REVELATION   אהבה רבה

אַהֲבָה רַבָּה אֲהַבְתָּנוּ, יי אֱלֹהֵינוּ, חֶמְלָה גְדוֹלָה וִיתֵרָה
חָמַלְתָּ עָלֵינוּ. אָבִינוּ מַלְכֵּנוּ, בַּעֲבוּר אֲבוֹתֵינוּ וְאִמּוֹתֵינוּ
שֶׁבָּטְחוּ בְךָ וַתְּלַמְּדֵם חֻקֵּי חַיִּים, כֵּן תְּחָנֵּנוּ וּתְלַמְּדֵנוּ.
אָבִינוּ, הָאָב הָרַחֲמָן, הַמְרַחֵם, רַחֵם עָלֵינוּ וְתֵן בְּלִבֵּנוּ
לְהָבִין וּלְהַשְׂכִּיל, לִשְׁמֹעַ, לִלְמֹד וּלְלַמֵּד, לִשְׁמֹר וְלַעֲשׂוֹת
וּלְקַיֵּם אֶת־כָּל־דִּבְרֵי תַלְמוּד תּוֹרָתֶךָ בְּאַהֲבָה.
וְהָאֵר עֵינֵינוּ בְּתוֹרָתֶךָ, וְדַבֵּק לִבֵּנוּ בְּמִצְוֹתֶיךָ, וְיַחֵד לְבָבֵנוּ
לְאַהֲבָה וּלְיִרְאָה אֶת־שְׁמֶךָ. וְלֹא־נֵבוֹשׁ לְעוֹלָם וָעֶד,
כִּי בְשֵׁם קָדְשְׁךָ הַגָּדוֹל וְהַנּוֹרָא בָּטָחְנוּ. נָגִילָה וְנִשְׂמְחָה
בִּישׁוּעָתֶךָ, כִּי אֵל פּוֹעֵל יְשׁוּעוֹת אָתָּה, וּבָנוּ בָחַרְתָּ וְקֵרַבְתָּנוּ
לְשִׁמְךָ הַגָּדוֹל סֶלָה בֶּאֱמֶת, לְהוֹדוֹת לְךָ וּלְיַחֶדְךָ בְּאַהֲבָה.
בָּרוּךְ אַתָּה יי, הַבּוֹחֵר בְּעַמּוֹ יִשְׂרָאֵל בְּאַהֲבָה.

*Deep is Your love for us, abiding Your compassion. From of old
we have put our trust in You, and You have taught us the laws of
life. Be gracious now to us, that we may understand and fulfill the
teachings of Your word.*

*Enlighten our eyes in Your Torah, that we may cling to Your
Mitzvot. Unite our hearts to love and revere Your name.*

*We trust in You and rejoice in Your saving power, for You are the
Source of our help. You have called us and drawn us near to You
in faithfulness.*

*Joyfully we lift up our voices and proclaim Your unity, O God.
In love, You have called us to Your service!*

❖ ❖

שְׁמַע יִשְׂרָאֵל: יהוה אֱלֹהֵינוּ, יהוה אֶחָד!

Sh'ma Yis-ra-eil: Adonai Eh-lo-hei-nu, Adonai Eh-chad!

Hear, O Israel: the Eternal One is our God,
the Eternal God alone!

בָּרוּךְ שֵׁם כְּבוֹד מַלְכוּתוֹ לְעוֹלָם וָעֶד!

Ba-ruch sheim k'vod mal-chu-toh l'o-lam va-ed!

Blessed is God's glorious majesty for ever and ever!

All are seated

וְאָהַבְתָּ אֵת יהוה אֱלֹהֶיךָ בְּכָל־לְבָבְךָ וּבְכָל־נַפְשְׁךָ
וּבְכָל־מְאֹדֶךָ: וְהָיוּ הַדְּבָרִים הָאֵלֶּה אֲשֶׁר אָנֹכִי מְצַוְּךָ
הַיּוֹם עַל־לְבָבֶךָ: וְשִׁנַּנְתָּם לְבָנֶיךָ וְדִבַּרְתָּ בָּם בְּשִׁבְתְּךָ
בְּבֵיתֶךָ וּבְלֶכְתְּךָ בַדֶּרֶךְ וּבְשָׁכְבְּךָ וּבְקוּמֶךָ: וּקְשַׁרְתָּם
לְאוֹת עַל־יָדֶךָ וְהָיוּ לְטֹטָפֹת בֵּין עֵינֶיךָ: וּכְתַבְתָּם
עַל־מְזֻזוֹת בֵּיתֶךָ וּבִשְׁעָרֶיךָ:

לְמַעַן תִּזְכְּרוּ וַעֲשִׂיתֶם אֶת־כָּל־מִצְוֹתָי וִהְיִיתֶם קְדֹשִׁים
לֵאלֹהֵיכֶם: אֲנִי יהוה אֱלֹהֵיכֶם אֲשֶׁר הוֹצֵאתִי אֶתְכֶם
מֵאֶרֶץ מִצְרַיִם לִהְיוֹת לָכֶם לֵאלֹהִים אֲנִי יהוה אֱלֹהֵיכֶם:

V'a-hav-ta et Adonai Eh-lo-heh-cha
b'chol l'va-v'cha u-v'chol naf-sh'cha u-v'chol m'o-deh-cha.
V'ha-yu ha-d'va-rim ha-ei-leh
a-sher a-no-chi m'tza-v'cha ha-yom al l'va-veh-cha.
V'shi-nan-tam l'va-neh-cha v'di-bar-ta bam
b'shiv-t'cha b'vei-teh-cha u-v'lech-t'cha va-deh-rech
u-v'shoch-b'cha u-v'ku-meh-cha. U-k'shar-tam l'oht al ya-deh-cha
v'ha-yu l'toh-ta-foht bein ei-neh-cha;
uch'tav-tam al m'zu-zoht bei-teh-cha u-vi-sh'a-reh-cha.

L'ma-an tiz-k'ru va-a-si-tem et kol mitz-vo-tai,
vi-h'yi-tem k'doh-shim lei-lo-hei-chem.
A-ni Adonai Eh-lo-hei-chem
a-sher ho-tzei-ti et-chem mei-eh-retz mitz-ra-yim
li-h'yoht la-chem lei-lo-him.
A-ni Adonai Eh-lo-hei-chem.

You shall love the Eternal One, your God, with all your heart, with all your mind, with all your being. Set these words, which I command you this day, upon your heart. Teach them faithfully to your children; speak of them in your home and on your way, when you lie down and when you rise up. Bind them as a sign upon your hand; let them be a symbol before your eyes; inscribe them on the doorposts of your house, and on your gates.

Be mindful of all My Mitzvot, and do them: so shall you consecrate yourselves to your God. I am your Eternal God who led you out of Egypt to be your God; I am your Eternal God.

REDEMPTION   גאולה

Eternal truth it is that You alone are God,
and there is none else.
May the righteous of all nations rejoice in Your love and exult in Your justice.

Let them beat their swords into plowshares;
let them beat their spears into pruninghooks.

Let nation not lift up sword against nation;
let them study war no more.
You shall not hate another in your heart; you shall love your neighbor as yourself.

Let the stranger in your midst be to you as the native;
for you were strangers in the land of Egypt.

From the house of bondage we went forth to freedom;
so let all be free to sing with joy:

מִי־כָמְכָה בָּאֵלִם, יהוה? מִי כָּמְכָה, נֶאְדָּר בַּקֹּדֶשׁ,
נוֹרָא תְהִלֹּת, עֹשֵׂה פֶלֶא?

שִׁירָה חֲדָשָׁה שִׁבְּחוּ גְאוּלִים לְשִׁמְךָ עַל־שְׂפַת הַיָּם;
יַחַד כֻּלָּם הוֹדוּ וְהִמְלִיכוּ וְאָמְרוּ: יי יִמְלֹךְ לְעוֹלָם וָעֶד!

צוּר יִשְׂרָאֵל, קוּמָה בְּעֶזְרַת יִשְׂרָאֵל,
וּפְדֵה כִנְאֻמֶךָ יְהוּדָה וְיִשְׂרָאֵל.
גֹּאֲלֵנוּ יי צְבָאוֹת שְׁמוֹ, קְדוֹשׁ יִשְׂרָאֵל.
בָּרוּךְ אַתָּה יי, גָּאַל יִשְׂרָאֵל.

Mi cha-mo-cha ba-ei-lim, Adonai?
Mi ka-mo-cha, neh-dar ba-ko-desh,
no-ra t'hi-loht, o-sei feh-leh?

Shi-ra cha-da-sha shi-b'chu g'u-lim l'shi-m'cha al s'fat ha-yam;
ya-chad ku-lam ho-du v'him-li-chu v'a-m'ru:
Adonai yim-loch l'o-lam va-ed!

Tsur Yis-ra-eil, ku-ma b'ez-rat Yis-ra-eil,
u-f'dei chi-n'u-me-cha Y'hu-dah v'yis-ra-eil.

Go-a-lei-nu Adonai ts'va-ot sh'mo,
k'dosh Yis-ra-eil.
Ba-ruch a-tah, Adonai, ga-al Yis-ra-eil.

Who is like You, Eternal One, among the gods that are worshipped?
Who is like You, majestic in holiness, awesome in splendor, doing
wonders?

A new song the redeemed sang to Your name. At the shore of the sea,
saved from destruction, they proclaimed Your sovereign power: The
Eternal One will reign for ever and ever!

O Rock of Israel, come to Israel's help. Fulfill Your promise of
redemption for Judah and Israel. Our Redeemer is God on High, the
Holy One of Israel. We praise You, O God, Redeemer of Israel.

70

T'filah תפלה

All rise

אֲדֹנָי, שְׂפָתַי תִּפְתָּח וּפִי יַגִּיד תְּהִלָּתֶךָ.

Eternal God, open my lips, that my mouth may declare Your glory.

GOD OF ALL GENERATIONS   אבות ואמהות

בָּרוּךְ אַתָּה יי, אֱלֹהֵינוּ וֵאלֹהֵי אֲבוֹתֵינוּ וְאִמּוֹתֵינוּ:
אֱלֹהֵי אַבְרָהָם, אֱלֹהֵי יִצְחָק, וֵאלֹהֵי יַעֲקֹב.
אֱלֹהֵי שָׂרָה, אֱלֹהֵי רִבְקָה, אֱלֹהֵי לֵאָה, וֵאלֹהֵי רָחֵל.
הָאֵל הַגָּדוֹל הַגִּבּוֹר וְהַנּוֹרָא, אֵל עֶלְיוֹן, גּוֹמֵל חֲסָדִים
טוֹבִים וְקוֹנֵה הַכֹּל, וְזוֹכֵר חַסְדֵי אָבוֹת וְאִמָּהוֹת,
וּמֵבִיא גְאֻלָּה לִבְנֵי בְנֵיהֶם, לְמַעַן שְׁמוֹ בְּאַהֲבָה.
מֶלֶךְ עוֹזֵר וּמוֹשִׁיעַ וּמָגֵן.
בָּרוּךְ אַתָּה יי, מָגֵן אַבְרָהָם וְעֶזְרַת שָׂרָה.

Ba-ruch a-ta Adonai,
Eh-lo-hei-nu vei-lo-hei a-vo-tei-nu v'i-mo-tei-nu:
Eh-lo-hei Av-ra-ham, Eh-lo-hei Yitz-chak, vei-lo-hei Ya-a-kov.
Eh-lo-hei Sa-rah, Eh-lo-hei Riv-kah,
Eh-lo-hei Lei-ah, vei-lo-hei Ra-cheil.
Ha-eil ha-ga-dol ha-gi-bor v'ha-no-ra, Eil el-yon,
go-meil cha-sa-dim toh-vim, v'ko-nei ha-kol,
v'zo-cheir chas-dei a-voht v'i-ma-hoht,
u-mei-vi g'u-la li-v'nei v'nei-hem, l'ma-an sh'mo, b'a-ha-va.
Meh-lech o-zeir u-mo-shi-a u-ma-gein.
Ba-ruch a-ta Adonai, ma-gein Av-ra-ham v'ez-rat Sa-rah.

Praised be our God, the God of our fathers and our mothers:
God of Abraham, God of Isaac, and God of Jacob;
God of Sarah, God of Rebekah,
God of Leah and God of Rachel;
great, mighty, and awesome God, God supreme.

71

Ruler of all the living, Your ways are ways of love.
You remember the faithfulness of our ancestors,
and in love bring redemption to their children's children
for the sake of Your name.
You are our Sovereign and our Help,
our Redeemer and our Shield.
We praise You, O God, Shield of Abraham, Protector of Sarah.

GOD'S POWER   גבורות

אַתָּה גִּבּוֹר לְעוֹלָם, אֲדֹנָי, מְחַיֵּה הַכֹּל אַתָּה, רַב לְהוֹשִׁיעַ.

מְכַלְכֵּל חַיִּים בְּחֶסֶד, מְחַיֵּה הַכֹּל בְּרַחֲמִים רַבִּים.

סוֹמֵךְ נוֹפְלִים, וְרוֹפֵא חוֹלִים, וּמַתִּיר אֲסוּרִים,

וּמְקַיֵּם אֱמוּנָתוֹ לִישֵׁנֵי עָפָר. מִי כָמוֹךָ בַּעַל גְּבוּרוֹת,

וּמִי דּוֹמֶה לָּךְ, מֶלֶךְ מֵמִית וּמְחַיֶּה וּמַצְמִיחַ יְשׁוּעָה?

וְנֶאֱמָן אַתָּה לְהַחֲיוֹת הַכֹּל. בָּרוּךְ אַתָּה יי, מְחַיֵּה הַכֹּל.

A-ta gi-bor l'o-lam, Adonai, m'cha-yei ha-kol a-ta, rav l'ho-shi-a.
M'chal-keil cha-yim b'cheh-sed,
m'cha-yei ha-kol b'ra-cha-mim ra-bim.
So-meich no-f'lim, v'ro-fei cho-lim, u-ma-tir a-su-rim,
u-m'ka-yeim eh-mu-na-toh li-shei-nei a-far.
Mi cha-mo-cha ba-al g'vu-roht, u-mi doh-meh lach,
meh-lech mei-meet u-m'cha-yeh u-matz-mi-ach y'shu-a?
V'neh-eh-man a-ta l'ha-cha-yoht ha-kol.
Ba-ruch a-ta Adonai, m'cha-yei ha-kol.

Eternal is Your might, O God; all life is Your gift;
great is Your power to save!

With love You sustain the living,
with great compassion give life to all.
You send help to the falling and healing to the sick;
You bring freedom to the captive
and keep faith with those who sleep in the dust.

72

Who is like You, Mighty One?
Who is Your equal, Author of life and death,
Source of salvation?

We praise You, Eternal God, Source of life.

SANCTIFICATION   קדושה

נְקַדֵּשׁ אֶת־שִׁמְךָ בָּעוֹלָם, כְּשֵׁם שֶׁמַּקְדִּישִׁים אוֹתוֹ בִּשְׁמֵי
מָרוֹם, כַּכָּתוּב עַל־יַד נְבִיאֶךָ: וְקָרָא זֶה אֶל־זֶה וְאָמַר:

We sanctify Your name on earth, even as all things, to the ends
of time and space, proclaim Your holiness, and in the words of
the prophet we say:

קָדוֹשׁ, קָדוֹשׁ, קָדוֹשׁ יהוה צְבָאוֹת,
מְלֹא כָל־הָאָרֶץ כְּבוֹדוֹ.

Ka-dosh, ka-dosh, ka-dosh Adonai tz'va-oht,
m'lo chol ha-a-retz k'vo-doh.

Holy, holy, holy is the Eternal One, God of the Hosts of Heaven!
The whole earth is ablaze with Your glory!

אַדִּיר אַדִּירֵנוּ, יי אֲדֹנֵינוּ, מָה־אַדִּיר שִׁמְךָ בְּכָל־הָאָרֶץ!

Source of our strength, Sovereign God, how majestic is Your
name in all the earth!

בָּרוּךְ כְּבוֹד־יהוה מִמְּקוֹמוֹ.

Ba-ruch k'vod Adonai mim-ko-mo.

Praised be the glory of God in heaven and earth.

אֶחָד הוּא אֱלֹהֵינוּ, הוּא אָבִינוּ, הוּא מַלְכֵּנוּ, הוּא מוֹשִׁיעֵנוּ;
וְהוּא יַשְׁמִיעֵנוּ בְּרַחֲמָיו לְעֵינֵי כָּל־חָי:

You alone are our God and our Creator; You are our Ruler and
our Helper; and in Your mercy You reveal Yourself in the sight
of all the living:

73

"I am the Eternal God!"   "אֲנִי יי אֱלֹהֵיכֶם!"

יִמְלֹךְ יהוה לְעוֹלָם, אֱלֹהַיִךְ צִיּוֹן, לְדֹר וָדֹר. הַלְלוּיָהּ!

Yim-loch Adonai l'o-lam, Eh-lo-ha-yich Tzi-yon,
l'dor va-dor. Ha-l'lu-yah!

The Eternal One shall reign for ever; your God, O Zion, from
generation to generation. Halleluyah!

לְדוֹר וָדוֹר נַגִּיד גָּדְלֶךָ, וּלְנֵצַח נְצָחִים קְדֻשָּׁתְךָ נַקְדִּישׁ.
וְשִׁבְחֲךָ, אֱלֹהֵינוּ, מִפִּינוּ לֹא יָמוּשׁ לְעוֹלָם וָעֶד.
בָּרוּךְ אַתָּה יי, הָאֵל הַקָּדוֹשׁ.

To all generations we will make known Your greatness, and to
all eternity proclaim Your holiness. Your praise, O God, shall
never depart from our lips.
We praise You, Eternal One, the holy God.

All are seated

THE HOLINESS OF SHABBAT   קדושת היום

Our God and God of all Israel, grant that our worship on this
Sabbath may be acceptable in Your sight. Sanctify us with Your
Mitzvot that we may share in the blessings of Your word. Teach us
to be satisfied with the gifts of Your goodness and gratefully to
rejoice in all Your mercies. Purify our hearts that we may serve
You in truth. O help us to preserve the Sabbath from generation to
generation, that it may bring rest and joy, peace and comfort to
the dwellings of our people, and through it Your name be hallowed
in all the earth. We thank You, O God, for the Sabbath and its
holiness.

MOST PRECIOUS OF DAYS   יִשְׂמְחוּ

יִשְׂמְחוּ בְמַלְכוּתְךָ שׁוֹמְרֵי שַׁבָּת וְקוֹרְאֵי עֹנֶג. עַם מְקַדְּשֵׁי
שְׁבִיעִי כֻּלָּם יִשְׂבְּעוּ וְיִתְעַנְּגוּ מִטּוּבֶךָ. וְהַשְּׁבִיעִי רָצִיתָ בּוֹ
וְקִדַּשְׁתּוֹ. חֶמְדַּת יָמִים אוֹתוֹ קָרָאתָ, זֵכֶר לְמַעֲשֵׂה בְרֵאשִׁית.

Yis-m'chu v'ma-l'chu-t'cha sho-m'rei, sha-bat v'ko-r'ei o-neg.
Am m'ka-d'shei sh'vi-i ku-lam yis-b'u v'yit-a-n'gu mi-tu-ve-cha.
V'hash'vi-i ra-tzi-ta bo v'ki-dash-to.
Chem-dat ya-mim o-to ka-ra-ta, zei-cher l'ma-a-sei v'rei-sheet.

Those who keep the Sabbath and call it a delight shall rejoice in Your Presence. All who hallow the seventh day shall be gladdened by Your goodness. This day is Israel's festival of the spirit, sanctified and blessed by You, the most precious of days, a symbol of the joy of creation.

WORSHIP   עבודה

רְצֵה, יי אֱלֹהֵינוּ, בְּעַמְּךָ יִשְׂרָאֵל, וּתְפִלָּתָם בְּאַהֲבָה תְקַבֵּל,
וּתְהִי לְרָצוֹן תָּמִיד עֲבוֹדַת יִשְׂרָאֵל עַמֶּךָ.
בָּרוּךְ אַתָּה יי, שֶׁאוֹתְךָ לְבַדְּךָ בְּיִרְאָה נַעֲבוֹד.

O God, look with favor upon us, and may our service be acceptable to You. We praise You, O God, whom alone we serve with reverence.

MEDITATION

We give thanks for the freedom that is ours, and we pray for those in other lands who are persecuted and oppressed. Help them to bear their burdens and keep alive in them the love of freedom and the hope of deliverance. Uphold also the hands of our brothers and sisters in the land of Israel, Your word from the tents of Jacob. We praise You, O God whose presence gives life to our people Israel.

TO WHOM OUR THANKS ARE DUE   הודאה

מוֹדִים אֲנַחְנוּ לָךְ, שָׁאַתָּה הוּא יי אֱלֹהֵינוּ וֵאלֹהֵי אֲבוֹתֵינוּ
וְאִמּוֹתֵינוּ לְעוֹלָם וָעֶד. צוּר חַיֵּינוּ, מָגֵן יִשְׁעֵנוּ, אַתָּה הוּא
לְדוֹר וָדוֹר. נוֹדֶה לְּךָ וּנְסַפֵּר תְּהִלָּתֶךָ, עַל־חַיֵּינוּ הַמְּסוּרִים
בְּיָדֶךָ, וְעַל־נִשְׁמוֹתֵינוּ הַפְּקוּדוֹת לָךְ, וְעַל־נִסֶּיךָ שֶׁבְּכָל־יוֹם
עִמָּנוּ, וְעַל־נִפְלְאוֹתֶיךָ וְטוֹבוֹתֶיךָ שֶׁבְּכָל־עֵת, עֶרֶב וָבֹקֶר
וְצָהֳרָיִם. הַטּוֹב: כִּי לֹא־כָלוּ רַחֲמֶיךָ, וְהַמְרַחֵם: כִּי־לֹא
תַמּוּ חֲסָדֶיךָ, מֵעוֹלָם קִוִּינוּ לָךְ. וְעַל כֻּלָּם יִתְבָּרַךְ וְיִתְרוֹמַם
שִׁמְךָ, מַלְכֵּנוּ, תָּמִיד לְעוֹלָם וָעֶד. וְכֹל הַחַיִּים יוֹדֽוּךָ סֶּלָה,
וִיהַלְלוּ אֶת שִׁמְךָ בֶּאֱמֶת, הָאֵל יְשׁוּעָתֵנוּ וְעֶזְרָתֵנוּ סֶלָה.
בָּרוּךְ אַתָּה, יי, הַטּוֹב שִׁמְךָ וּלְךָ נָאֶה לְהוֹדוֹת.

*We gratefully acknowledge, Eternal God, that You are our Creator
and Preserver, the Rock of our life and our protecting Shield.*

*We give thanks to You for our lives which are in Your hand, for our
souls which are ever in Your keeping, for Your wondrous
providence and Your continuous goodness, which You bestow upon
us day by day. Truly, Your mercies never fail, and Your love and
kindness never cease. Therefore do we put our trust in You.
Blessed is the Eternal God, to whom our thanks are due.*

PEACE   ברכת שלום

שִׂים שָׁלוֹם, טוֹבָה וּבְרָכָה, חֵן וָחֶסֶד וְרַחֲמִים,
עָלֵינוּ וְעַל־כָּל־יִשְׂרָאֵל עַמֶּךָ.
בָּרְכֵנוּ אָבִינוּ, כֻּלָּנוּ כְּאֶחָד, בְּאוֹר פָּנֶיךָ,
כִּי בְאוֹר פָּנֶיךָ נָתַתָּ לָּנוּ, יי אֱלֹהֵינוּ,
תּוֹרַת חַיִּים, וְאַהֲבַת חֶסֶד,
וּצְדָקָה וּבְרָכָה וְרַחֲמִים, וְחַיִּים וְשָׁלוֹם.

וְטוֹב בְּעֵינֶיךָ לְבָרֵךְ אֶת־עַמְּךָ יִשְׂרָאֵל
בְּכָל־עֵת וּבְכָל־שָׁעָה בִּשְׁלוֹמֶךָ.
בָּרוּךְ אַתָּה יי, הַמְבָרֵךְ אֶת־עַמּוֹ יִשְׂרָאֵל בַּשָּׁלוֹם.

Sim sha-lom to-vah uv'ra-cha chein va-che-sed v'ra-cha-mim
a-lei-nu v'al kol Yis-ra-eil a-me-cha.

Ba-r'chei-nu a-vi-nu ku-la-nu k'e-chad b'or pa-ne-cha
ki b'or pa-ne-cha na-ta-ta la-nu, Adonai Eh-lo-hei-nu,
to-rat cha-yim v'a-ha-vat che-sed
u-tz'da-ka u-v'ra-chah v'ra-cha-mim v'cha-yim v'sha-lom.

V'tov b'ei-neh-cha l'va-reich et a-m'cha Yis-ra-eil
b'chol eit u-v'chol sha-ah bi-sh'lo-meh-cha.
Ba-ruch a-ta Adonai,
ha-m'va-reich et a-mo Yis-ra-eil ba-sha-lom.

Grant us peace, Your most precious gift,
O Eternal Source of peace,
and give us the will to proclaim its message
to all the peoples of the earth.

Bless our country, that it may always be a stronghold of peace,
and its advocate among the nations.

May contentment reign within its borders,
health and happiness within its homes.

Strengthen the bonds of friendship
among the inhabitants of all lands,
and may the love of Your name hallow
every home and every heart.

We praise You, O God, the Source of peace.

SILENT PRAYER

אֱלֹהַי, נְצֹר לְשׁוֹנִי מֵרָע, וּשְׂפָתַי מִדַּבֵּר מִרְמָה. וְלִמְקַלְלַי
נַפְשִׁי תִדּוֹם וְנַפְשִׁי כֶּעָפָר לַכֹּל תִּהְיֶה. פְּתַח לִבִּי בְּתוֹרָתֶךָ,
וּבְמִצְוֹתֶיךָ תִּרְדּוֹף נַפְשִׁי. וְכָל־הַחוֹשְׁבִים עָלַי רָעָה, מְהֵרָה
הָפֵר עֲצָתָם וְקַלְקֵל מַחֲשַׁבְתָּם. עֲשֵׂה לְמַעַן שְׁמֶךָ, עֲשֵׂה
לְמַעַן יְמִינֶךָ, עֲשֵׂה לְמַעַן קְדֻשָּׁתֶךָ, עֲשֵׂה לְמַעַן תּוֹרָתֶךָ;
לְמַעַן יֵחָלְצוּן יְדִידֶיךָ, הוֹשִׁיעָה יְמִינְךָ וַעֲנֵנִי.

O God, keep my tongue from evil and my lips from deceit. Help
me to be silent in the face of derision, humble in the presence of
all. Open my heart to Your Torah, and I will hasten to do Your
Mitzvot. Save me with Your power; in time of trouble be my
answer, that those who love You may rejoice.

❖ ❖

יִהְיוּ לְרָצוֹן אִמְרֵי־פִי וְהֶגְיוֹן לִבִּי לְפָנֶיךָ, יְהוָה, צוּרִי וְגֹאֲלִי.

Yi-h'yu l'ra-tson i-m'rei fi v'heg-yon li-bi l'fa-ne-cha,
Adonai tsu-ri v'go-a-li.

May the words of my mouth, and the meditations of my heart,
be acceptable to You, O God, my Rock and my Redeemer.

❖

עֹשֶׂה שָׁלוֹם בִּמְרוֹמָיו, הוּא יַעֲשֶׂה שָׁלוֹם
עָלֵינוּ וְעַל־כָּל־יִשְׂרָאֵל, וְאִמְרוּ אָמֵן.

O-seh sha-lom bi-m'ro-mav, hu ya-a-seh sha-lom
a-lei-nu v'al kol Yis-ra-eil, v'i-m'ru: A-mein.

May the One who causes peace to reign in the high heavens
let peace descend on us, on all Israel, and all the world.

The Torah Service begins on page 79

Aleinu is on page 85

For the Reading of Torah
סדר קריאת התורה

Assembled at a mountain,
our people,
still bent from oppression,
found You,
found Your Torah,
found Your truth,
and embraced the destiny
that has shaped worlds.

Help us still to shape the world
according to Your will,
that this world
may reveal itself to You
as You have revealed Yourself to our people:
in love.

All rise

ARK IS OPENED

שְׂאוּ שְׁעָרִים רָאשֵׁיכֶם, וְהִנָּשְׂאוּ פִּתְחֵי עוֹלָם,
וְיָבוֹא מֶלֶךְ הַכָּבוֹד! מִי הוּא זֶה מֶלֶךְ הַכָּבוֹד?
יהוה צְבָאוֹת—הוּא מֶלֶךְ הַכָּבוֹד! סֶלָה.

S'u sh'a-rim ra-shei-chem
v'hi-nas'u pit'chei o-lam
v'ya-vo meh-lech ha-ka-vod.
Mi hu zeh meh-lech ha-ka-vod?
Adonai tz'va-ot hu meh-lech ha-ka-vod.
Se-lah!

❖

79

עַל־שְׁלשָׁה דְבָרִים הָעוֹלָם עוֹמֵד:
עַל הַתּוֹרָה, וְעַל הָעֲבוֹדָה, וְעַל גְּמִילוּת חֲסָדִים.

Al sh'lo-shah d'va-rim ha-o-lam o-meid:
Al ha-to-rah, v'al ha-a-vo-dah, v'al g'mi-lut cha-sa-dim.

❖ ❖

בֵּית יַעֲקֹב, לְכוּ וְנֵלְכָה בְּאוֹר יהוה:

O House of Israel, come, let us walk by the light of our God.

שְׁמַע יִשְׂרָאֵל: יהוה אֱלֹהֵינוּ, יהוה אֶחָד!

Hear, O Israel: the Eternal One is our God,
the Eternal God alone!

אֶחָד אֱלֹהֵינוּ, גָּדוֹל אֲדוֹנֵינוּ, קָדוֹשׁ שְׁמוֹ.

Our God is One; great and holy is the Eternal One.

גַּדְּלוּ לַיהוה אִתִּי וּנְרוֹמְמָה שְׁמוֹ יַחְדָּו.

O magnify the Eternal One with me, and together let us exalt God's name.

HAKAFAH — PROCESSION WITH THE SCROLL

לְךָ, יהוה, הַגְּדֻלָּה וְהַגְּבוּרָה וְהַתִּפְאֶרֶת וְהַנֵּצַח וְהַהוֹד,
כִּי כֹל בַּשָּׁמַיִם וּבָאָרֶץ.
לְךָ יהוה הַמַּמְלָכָה וְהַמִּתְנַשֵּׂא לְכֹל לְרֹאשׁ.

Yours, O God, is the greatness, the power, the glory, the victory, and the majesty, for all that is in heaven and earth is Yours. You, O God, are sovereign; You are supreme over all.

❖

80

לֹא יִשָּׂא גוֹי אֶל גוֹי חֶֽרֶב, לֹא יִלְמְדוּ עוֹד מִלְחָמָה.

Lo yi-sa goi el goi che-rev, lo yil-m'du od mil-cha-ma.

❖

יִשְׂמְחוּ הַשָּׁמַֽיִם וְתָגֵל הָאָֽרֶץ. יִרְעַם הַיָּם וּמְלֹאוֹ.

Yis-m'chu ha-sha-ma-yim v'ta-geil ha-a-retz. Yir-am ha-yam u-m'lo-o.

All are seated

Reading of the Torah

BEFORE THE READING

בָּרְכוּ אֶת־יִי הַמְבֹרָךְ!

בָּרוּךְ יִי הַמְבֹרָךְ לְעוֹלָם וָעֶד!

בָּרוּךְ אַתָּה יִי, אֱלֹהֵֽינוּ מֶֽלֶךְ הָעוֹלָם,

אֲשֶׁר בָּֽחַר־בָּֽנוּ מִכָּל־הָעַמִּים וְנָֽתַן־לָֽנוּ אֶת־תּוֹרָתוֹ.

בָּרוּךְ אַתָּה יִי, נוֹתֵן הַתּוֹרָה.

Praise the One to whom our praise is due!

Praised be the One to whom our praise is due, now and for ever!

We praise You, Eternal God, Sovereign of the universe:
You have chosen us from all peoples by giving us the Torah.
We praise You, O God, Giver of the Torah.

AFTER THE READING

בָּרוּךְ אַתָּה יִי, אֱלֹהֵֽינוּ מֶֽלֶךְ הָעוֹלָם,

אֲשֶׁר נָֽתַן לָֽנוּ תּוֹרַת אֱמֶת וְחַיֵּי עוֹלָם נָטַע בְּתוֹכֵֽנוּ.

בָּרוּךְ אַתָּה יִי, נוֹתֵן הַתּוֹרָה.

We praise You, Eternal God, Sovereign of the universe:
You have given us a Torah of truth, implanting within us eternal life.
We praise You, O God, Giver of the Torah.

81

READING THE TORAH

HAGBA-HA — LIFTING THE TORAH

All rise

וְזֹאת הַתּוֹרָה אֲשֶׁר־שָׂם מֹשֶׁה לִפְנֵי בְּנֵי יִשְׂרָאֵל,
עַל־פִּי יי בְּיַד־מֹשֶׁה.

Ve'zot ha-to-rah a-sher sam Mo-sheh lif-nei b'nei Yis-ra-eil
al pi Adonai b'yad Mo-sheh

This is the Torah that Moses placed before the people of Israel.

All are seated

Reading of the Haftarah

BEFORE THE READING

בָּרוּךְ אַתָּה יי, אֱלֹהֵינוּ מֶלֶךְ הָעוֹלָם, אֲשֶׁר בָּחַר בִּנְבִיאִים
טוֹבִים וְרָצָה בְדִבְרֵיהֶם הַנֶּאֱמָרִים בֶּאֱמֶת. בָּרוּךְ אַתָּה יי,
הַבּוֹחֵר בַּתּוֹרָה וּבְמֹשֶׁה עַבְדּוֹ וּבְיִשְׂרָאֵל עַמּוֹ וּבִנְבִיאֵי
הָאֱמֶת וָצֶדֶק.

We praise You, Eternal God, Sovereign of the universe: You have called
faithful prophets to speak words of truth. We praise You for the revelation
of Torah, for Moses Your servant and Israel Your people, and for the
prophets of truth and righteousness.

AFTER THE READING

בָּרוּךְ אַתָּה יי, אֱלֹהֵינוּ מֶלֶךְ הָעוֹלָם, צוּר כָּל־הָעוֹלָמִים,
צַדִּיק בְּכָל־הַדּוֹרוֹת, הָאֵל הַנֶּאֱמָן, הָאוֹמֵר וְעוֹשֶׂה, הַמְדַבֵּר
וּמְקַיֵּם, שֶׁכָּל־דְּבָרָיו אֱמֶת וָצֶדֶק.

עַל־הַתּוֹרָה וְעַל־הָעֲבוֹדָה וְעַל־הַנְּבִיאִים וְעַל־יוֹם הַשַּׁבָּת
הַזֶּה, שֶׁנָּתַתָּ־לָנוּ, יי אֱלֹהֵינוּ, לִקְדֻשָּׁה וְלִמְנוּחָה, לְכָבוֹד

וּלְתִפְאָרֶת, עַל־הַכֹּל, יי אֱלֹהֵינוּ, אֲנַחְנוּ מוֹדִים לָךְ,
וּמְבָרְכִים אוֹתָךְ. יִתְבָּרַךְ שִׁמְךָ בְּפִי כָּל־חַי תָּמִיד
לְעוֹלָם וָעֶד. בָּרוּךְ אַתָּה יי, מְקַדֵּשׁ הַשַּׁבָּת.

We praise You, Eternal God, Sovereign of the universe, the Rock of all creation, the Righteous One of all generations, the faithful God whose word is deed, whose every command is just and true.

For the Torah, for the privilege of worship, for the prophets, and for this Shabbat that You, our Eternal God, have given us for holiness and rest, for honor and glory, we thank and praise You. May Your name be praised for ever by every living being. We praise You, O God, for Shabbat and its holiness.

Returning the Torah to the Ark

All rise

יְהַלְלוּ אֶת־שֵׁם יהוה, כִּי נִשְׂגָּב שְׁמוֹ לְבַדּוֹ.

Let us praise the Eternal God, whose name alone is exalted.

הוֹדוֹ עַל אֶרֶץ וְשָׁמָיִם, וַיָּרֶם קֶרֶן לְעַמּוֹ, תְּהִלָּה
לְכָל־חֲסִידָיו, לִבְנֵי יִשְׂרָאֵל עַם קְרוֹבוֹ. הַלְלוּיָהּ!

Your splendor covers heaven and earth; You are the strength of Your people, making glorious Your faithful ones, Israel, a people close to You. Halleluyah!

❖ ❖

God's Torah is perfect, reviving the soul;
God's teaching is sure, making wise the simple.

God's precepts are right, delighting the mind;
God's Mitzvah is clear, giving light to the eyes.

God's word is pure, enduring for ever;
God's judgments are true, and altogether just.

❖ ❖

Behold, a good doctrine has been given you, My Torah; do not forsake it. It is a tree of life to those who hold it fast, and all who cling to it find happiness. Its ways are ways of pleasantness, and all its paths are peace.

כִּי לֶקַח טוֹב נָתַתִּי לָכֶם, תּוֹרָתִי אַל־תַּעֲזֹבוּ.

עֵץ־חַיִּים הִיא לַמַּחֲזִיקִים בָּהּ, וְתֹמְכֶיהָ מְאֻשָּׁר.

דְּרָכֶיהָ דַרְכֵי־נֹעַם, וְכָל־נְתִיבוֹתֶיהָ שָׁלוֹם.

הֲשִׁיבֵנוּ יהוה אֵלֶיךָ, וְנָשׁוּבָה. חַדֵּשׁ יָמֵינוּ כְּקֶדֶם.

Eitz cha-yim hi la-ma-cha-zi-kim bah, v'to-m'che-ha m'u-shar.
D'ra-che-ha dar-chei no-am, v'chol n'ti-vo-te-ha sha-lom.

Ha-shi-vei-nu Adonai ei-le-cha, v'na-shu-va.
Cha-deish ya-mei-nu k'ke-dem.

Help us to return to You, O God; then truly shall we return.
Renew our days as in the past.

THE ARK IS CLOSED

Aleinu

עָלֵינוּ

All rise

עָלֵינוּ לְשַׁבֵּחַ לַאֲדוֹן הַכֹּל, לָתֵת גְּדֻלָּה לְיוֹצֵר בְּרֵאשִׁית,

שֶׁלֹּא עָשָׂנוּ כְּגוֹיֵי הָאֲרָצוֹת, וְלֹא שָׂמָנוּ כְּמִשְׁפְּחוֹת הָאֲדָמָה;

שֶׁלֹּא שָׂם חֶלְקֵנוּ כָּהֶם, וְגוֹרָלֵנוּ כְּכָל־הֲמוֹנָם.

וַאֲנַחְנוּ כּוֹרְעִים וּמִשְׁתַּחֲוִים וּמוֹדִים

לִפְנֵי מֶלֶךְ מַלְכֵי הַמְּלָכִים, הַקָּדוֹשׁ בָּרוּךְ הוּא.

A-lei-nu l'sha-bei-ach la-a-don ha-kol,
la-teit g'du-la l'yo-tzeir b'rei-sheet,
sheh-lo a-sa-nu k'go-yei ha-a-ra-tzot,
v'lo sa-ma-nu k'mish-p'chot ha-a-da-ma;
sheh-lo sam chel-kei-nu ka-hem, v'go-ra-lei-nu k'chol ha-mo-nam.

Va-a-nach-nu ko-r'im u-mish-ta-cha-vim u-mo-dim
li-f'nei meh-lech mal-chei ha-m'la-chim, ha-ka-dosh ba-ruch hu.

We must praise the God of all, the Maker of heaven and earth, who
has set us apart from the other families of earth, giving us a destiny
unique among the nations.

Therefore we bow in awe and thanksgiving before the One who is
sovereign over all, the Holy and Blessed One.

❖ ❖

שֶׁהוּא נוֹטֶה שָׁמַיִם וְיוֹסֵד אָרֶץ, וּמוֹשַׁב יְקָרוֹ בַּשָּׁמַיִם מִמַּעַל

וּשְׁכִינַת עֻזּוֹ בְּגָבְהֵי מְרוֹמִים. הוּא אֱלֹהֵינוּ, אֵין עוֹד.

אֱמֶת מַלְכֵּנוּ, אֶפֶס זוּלָתוֹ, כַּכָּתוּב בְּתוֹרָתוֹ:

וְיָדַעְתָּ הַיּוֹם וַהֲשֵׁבֹתָ אֶל־לְבָבֶךָ, כִּי יי הוּא הָאֱלֹהִים

בַּשָּׁמַיִם מִמַּעַל וְעַל־הָאָרֶץ מִתָּחַת, אֵין עוֹד.

Sheh-hu no-teh sha-ma-yim v'yo-seid a-retz,
u-mo-shav y'ka-ro ba-sha-ma-yim mi-ma-al
u-sh'chi-nat u-zo b'gov-hei m'ro-mim. Hu Eh-lo-hei-nu, ein od.
Eh-met mal-kei-nu, eh-fes zu-la-toh, ka-ka-tuv b'toh-ra-toh:
V'ya-da-ta ha-yom v'ha-shei-vo-ta el l'va-ve-cha,
ki A-do-nai hu ha-eh-lo-him ba-sha-ma-yim mi-ma-al
v'al ha-a-retz mi-ta-chat, ein od.

You spread out the heavens and established the earth; You are our God; there is none else. In truth You alone are our sovereign God, as it is written: "Know then this day and take it to heart: the Eternal One is God in the heavens above and on the earth below; there is none else."

Eternal God, we face the morrow with hope made stronger by the vision of Your deliverance, a world where poverty and war are banished, where injustice and hate are gone.

Teach us more and more to respond to the pain of others, to heed Your call for justice, to pursue the blessing of peace. Grant us wisdom and strength, O God, that we may bring nearer the day when all the world shall be one.

וְנֶאֱמַר: "וְהָיָה יהוה לְמֶלֶךְ עַל־כָּל־הָאָרֶץ;
בַּיּוֹם הַהוּא יִהְיֶה יהוה אֶחָד וּשְׁמוֹ אֶחָד."

V'neh-eh-mar: V'ha-yah Adonai l'meh-lech al kol ha-a-retz;
ba-yom ha-hu yi-h'yeh Adonai Eh-chad, u-sh'mo Eh-chad.

And it has been said: "The Eternal God shall rule over all the earth; On that day You shall be One and Your name shall be One."

❖ ❖

Our thoughts turn to those whose lives have been a blessing to humanity. We recall the loved ones whom death has recently taken from us. And we remember those who died at this season in years past, and those whom we have taken into our hearts with our own . . . . The memories of all of them are with us; our griefs and sympathies are mingled. Loving God, we praise Your name:

Mourner's Kaddish קדיש יתום

יִתְגַּדַּל וְיִתְקַדַּשׁ שְׁמֵהּ רַבָּא בְּעָלְמָא דִי־בְרָא כִרְעוּתֵהּ,
וְיַמְלִיךְ מַלְכוּתֵהּ בְּחַיֵּיכוֹן וּבְיוֹמֵיכוֹן וּבְחַיֵּי דְכָל־בֵּית
יִשְׂרָאֵל, בַּעֲגָלָא וּבִזְמַן קָרִיב, וְאִמְרוּ: אָמֵן.

Yit-ga-dal v'yit-ka-dash sh'mei ra-ba b'al-ma di-v'ra chir-u-tei,
v'yam-lich mal-chu-tei b'cha-yei-chon u-v'yo-mei-chon u-v'cha-yei
d'chol beit Yis-ra-eil, ba-a-ga-la u-viz-man ka-riv, v'i-m'ru: A-mein.

יְהֵא שְׁמֵהּ רַבָּא מְבָרַךְ לְעָלַם וּלְעָלְמֵי עָלְמַיָּא.

Y'hei sh'mei ra-ba m'va-rach l'a-lam u-l'al-mei al-ma-ya.

יִתְבָּרַךְ וְיִשְׁתַּבַּח, וְיִתְפָּאַר וְיִתְרוֹמַם וְיִתְנַשֵּׂא,
וְיִתְהַדָּר וְיִתְעַלֶּה וְיִתְהַלָּל שְׁמֵהּ דְּקוּדְשָׁא, בְּרִיךְ הוּא,

Yit-ba-rach v'yish-ta-bach v'yit-pa-ar, v'yit-ro-mam, v'yit-na-sei,
v'yit-ha-dar, v'yit-a-leh, v'yit-ha-lal sh'mei d'kud-sha, b'rich hu,

לְעֵלָּא מִן־כָּל־בִּרְכָתָא וְשִׁירָתָא, תֻּשְׁבְּחָתָא וְנֶחֱמָתָא
דַּאֲמִירָן בְּעָלְמָא, וְאִמְרוּ: אָמֵן.

L'ei-la min kol bir-cha-ta v'shi-ra-ta, tush-b'cha-ta v'neh-cheh-ma-ta
da-a-mi-ran b'al-ma, v'i-m'ru: A-mein.

יְהֵא שְׁלָמָא רַבָּא מִן־שְׁמַיָּא וְחַיִּים
עָלֵינוּ וְעַל־כָּל־יִשְׂרָאֵל, וְאִמְרוּ: אָמֵן.

Y'hei sh'la-ma ra-ba min sh'ma-ya v'cha-yim a-lei-nu v'al kol
Yis-ra-eil, v'i-m'ru: A-mein.

עֹשֶׂה שָׁלוֹם בִּמְרוֹמָיו, הוּא יַעֲשֶׂה שָׁלוֹם
עָלֵינוּ וְעַל־כָּל־יִשְׂרָאֵל, וְאִמְרוּ: אָמֵן.

O-seh sha-lom bi-m'ro-mav, hu ya-a-seh sha-lom
a-lei-nu v'al kol Yis-ra-eil, v'i-m'ru: A-mein.

Let the glory of God be extolled, and God's great name be hallowed in the world whose creation God willed. May God rule in our own day, in our own lives, and in the life of all Israel, and let us say: Amen.

Let God's great name be blessed for ever and ever.

Beyond all the praises, songs, and adorations that we can utter is the Holy One, the Blessed One, whom yet we glorify, honor, and exalt. And let us say: Amen.

For us and for all Israel, may the blessing of peace and the promise of life come true, and let us say: Amen.

May the One who causes peace to reign in the high heavens, let peace descend on us, on all Israel, and all the world, and let us say: Amen.

May the Source of peace send peace to all who mourn,
and comfort to all who are bereaved. *Amen.*

❖ ❖
❖

Kiddush for Shabbat Morning
קדוש לשחרית של שבת

וְשָׁמְרוּ בְנֵי־יִשְׂרָאֵל אֶת־הַשַּׁבָּת,
לַעֲשׂוֹת אֶת־הַשַּׁבָּת לְדֹרֹתָם בְּרִית עוֹלָם.
בֵּינִי וּבֵין בְּנֵי יִשְׂרָאֵל אוֹת הִיא לְעֹלָם
כִּי שֵׁשֶׁת יָמִים עָשָׂה יהוה אֶת־הַשָּׁמַיִם וְאֶת־הָאָרֶץ,
וּבַיּוֹם הַשְּׁבִיעִי שָׁבַת וַיִּנָּפַשׁ.

V'sha-m'ru v'nei Yis-ra-eil et ha-sha-bat,
la-a-sot et ha-sha-bat l'do-ro-tam b'rit o-lam.
Bei-ni u-vein b'nei Yis-ra-eil ot hi l'o-lam.
Ki shei-shet ya-mim a-sa Adonai et ha-sha-ma-yim v'et ha-a-retz,
u-va-yom ha-sh'vi-i sha-vat va-yi-na-fash.

The people of Israel shall keep Shabbat, observing Shabbat in every generation as a covenant for all time. It shall be a sign for ever between Me and the people of Israel, for in six days God made heaven and earth, and on the seventh day, God rested and was refreshed.

עַל־כֵּן בֵּרַךְ יהוה אֶת־יוֹם הַשַּׁבָּת וַיְקַדְּשֵׁהוּ.

Al kein bei-rach Adonai et yom ha-sha-bat va-y'kad-shei-hu.

Therefore the Eternal One blessed the seventh day
and called it holy.

בָּרוּךְ אַתָּה יי, אֱלֹהֵינוּ מֶלֶךְ הָעוֹלָם, בּוֹרֵא פְּרִי הַגָּפֶן.

Ba-ruch a-ta Adonai, Eh-lo-hei-nu meh-lech ha-o-lam,
bo-rei p'ri ha-ga-fen.

We praise You, Eternal God, Sovereign of the universe, Creator of the fruit of the vine.

89

Havdalah

הבדלה

As Shabbat ends, the Havdalah candle is kindled.
The following biblical verses may be read or chanted.
It is customary to lift the cup of wine or grape juice high when the last
sentence is read and then proceed directly to the blessing for wine.

הִנֵּה אֵל יְשׁוּעָתִי, אֶבְטַח וְלֹא אֶפְחָד.

כִּי עָזִּי וְזִמְרָת יָהּ יהוה, וַיְהִי־לִי לִישׁוּעָה.

וּשְׁאַבְתֶּם מַיִם בְּשָׂשׂוֹן מִמַּעַיְנֵי הַיְשׁוּעָה.

לַיהוה הַיְשׁוּעָה, עַל־עַמְּךָ בִרְכָתֶךָ, סֶּלָה.

יהוה צְבָאוֹת עִמָּנוּ, מִשְׂגָּב־לָנוּ אֱלֹהֵי יַעֲקֹב, סֶלָה.

יהוה צְבָאוֹת, אַשְׁרֵי אָדָם בֹּטֵחַ בָּךְ!

יהוה, הוֹשִׁיעָה; הַמֶּלֶךְ יַעֲנֵנוּ בְיוֹם־קָרְאֵנוּ.

לַיְּהוּדִים הָיְתָה אוֹרָה וְשִׂמְחָה, וְשָׂשׂוֹן וִיקָר; כֵּן תִּהְיֶה לָנוּ.

כּוֹס יְשׁוּעוֹת אֶשָּׂא, וּבְשֵׁם יהוה אֶקְרָא.

Hi-nei Eil y'shu-a-ti ev-tach, v'lo ef-chad.
Ki o-zi v'zim-rat Ya Adonai, va-y'hi li li-shu-a.

U-sh'av-tem ma-yim b'sa-son mi-ma-a-y'nei ha-y'shu-a.
La-a-do-nai ha-y'shu-a, al a-m'cha bir-cha-te-cha, se-la.

Adonai tz'va-ot i-ma-nu, mis-gav la-nu Eh-lo-hei Ya-a-kov, se-la.
Adonai tz'va-ot, ash-rei a-dam bo-tei-ach bach!

Adonai, ho-shi-a; ha-meh-lech ya-a-nei-nu v'yom kor-ei-nu

La-y'hu-dim ha-y'ta o-ra v'sim-cha, v'sa-son vi-kar;
kein ti-h'yeh la-nu. Kos y'shu-ot e-sa, u-v'sheim Adonai ek-ra.

Behold, God is my Help; trusting in the Eternal One, I am not afraid. For
the Eternal One is my strength and my song, and has become my
salvation. With joy we draw water from the wells of salvation. The Eternal
One brings deliverance, and blessing to the people. The God of the Hosts

of heaven is with us; the God of Jacob is our stronghold. God of the Hosts of heaven, happy is the one who trusts in You! Save us, Eternal One; answer us, when we call upon You. Give us light and joy, gladness and honor, as in the happiest days of our people's past. Then shall we lift up the cup to rejoice in Your saving power, and call out Your name in praise.

❖ ❖

THE WINE OR GRAPE JUICE

בָּרוּךְ אַתָּה יי, אֱלֹהֵינוּ מֶלֶךְ הָעוֹלָם, בּוֹרֵא פְּרִי הַגָּפֶן.

Ba-ruch a-ta A-do-nai, Eh-lo-hei-nu meh-lech ha-o-lam,
bo-rei p'ri ha-ga-fen.

We praise You, Eternal God, Sovereign of the universe: You create the fruit of the vine.

(The leader does not drink the wine or grape juice until after the final blessing, when Havdalah is fully complete.)

❖ ❖

THE SPICES

The leader holds up the spice box.

בָּרוּךְ אַתָּה יי, אֱלֹהֵינוּ מֶלֶךְ הָעוֹלָם, בּוֹרֵא מִינֵי בְשָׂמִים.

Ba-ruch a-ta Adonai, Eh-lo-hei-nu meh-lech ha-o-lam,
bo-rei mi-nei v'sa-mim.

We praise You, Eternal God, Sovereign of the universe, for all the world's spices.

The leader shakes the spices, smells them, and passes them on so that all may enjoy the fragrance.

❖ ❖

HAVDALAH

LIGHT

Raise the Havdalah candle

בָּרוּךְ אַתָּה יי, אֱלֹהֵינוּ מֶלֶךְ הָעוֹלָם, בּוֹרֵא מְאוֹרֵי הָאֵשׁ.

Ba-ruch a-ta Adonai, Eh-lo-hei-nu meh-lech ha-o-lam,
bo-rei m'o-rei ha-eish.

We praise You, Eternal God, Sovereign of the universe,
Creator of the light of fire.

❖ ❖

בָּרוּךְ אַתָּה יי, אֱלֹהֵינוּ מֶלֶךְ הָעוֹלָם, הַמַּבְדִּיל בֵּין קֹדֶשׁ
לְחוֹל, בֵּין אוֹר לְחֹשֶׁךְ, בֵּין יִשְׂרָאֵל לָעַמִּים,
בֵּין יוֹם הַשְּׁבִיעִי לְשֵׁשֶׁת יְמֵי הַמַּעֲשֶׂה.

בָּרוּךְ אַתָּה יי, הַמַּבְדִּיל בֵּין קֹדֶשׁ לְחוֹל.

We praise You, Eternal God, Sovereign of the universe: You
make distinctions, teaching us to distinguish the commonplace
from the holy; You create light and darkness, Israel and the
nations, the seventh day of rest and the six days of labor.

We praise You, O God:
You call us to distinguish the commonplace from the holy.

Sip the wine or grape juice.

*Extinguish the Havdalah candle in the remaining wine
while the following passages are sung or said.*

הַמַּבְדִּיל בֵּין קֹדֶשׁ לְחוֹל, חַטֹּאתֵינוּ הוּא יִמְחֹל,
זַרְעֵנוּ וְכַסְפֵּנוּ יַרְבֶּה כַחוֹל, וְכַכּוֹכָבִים בַּלָּיְלָה.

Ha-mav-dil bein ko-desh l'chol, cha-to-tei-nu hu yim-chol,
zar-ei-nu v'chas-pei-nu yar-beh ka-chol v'cha-ko-cha-vim ba-lai-la.

You teach us to distinguish between the commonplace and the holy: teach
us also to transform our sins to merits. Let those who love You be
numerous as the sands, and the stars of heaven.

HAVDALAH

Sha-vu-a tov...   ‎שָׁבוּעַ טוֹב...‎

A good week. A week of peace.
May gladness reign and joy increase.

❖ ❖

‎אֵלִיָּהוּ הַנָּבִיא, אֵלִיָּהוּ הַתִּשְׁבִּי;‎
‎אֵלִיָּהוּ הַגִּלְעָדִי.‎
‎בִּמְהֵרָה בְיָמֵינוּ, יָבֹא אֵלֵינוּ;‎
‎עִם מָשִׁיחַ בֶּן דָּוִד, אֵלִיָּהוּ...‎

Ei-li-ya-hu ha-na-vi, Ei-li-ya-hu ha-tish-bi;
Ei-li-ya-hu ha-gil-a-di.
Bi-m'hei-ra v'ya-mei-nu, ya-vo ei-lei-nu;
im ma-shi-ach ben Da-vid, Ei-li-ya-hu...

Songs

שירים

ADON OLAM

אדון עולם

בְּטֶרֶם כָּל־יְצִיר נִבְרָא,   אֲדוֹן עוֹלָם אֲשֶׁר מָלַךְ

אֲזַי מֶלֶךְ שְׁמוֹ נִקְרָא.   לְעֵת נַעֲשָׂה בְחֶפְצוֹ כֹּל,

לְבַדּוֹ יִמְלוֹךְ נוֹרָא,   וְאַחֲרֵי כִּכְלוֹת הַכֹּל,

וְהוּא יִהְיֶה בְּתִפְאָרָה.   וְהוּא הָיָה וְהוּא הֹוֶה,

לְהַמְשִׁיל לוֹ, לְהַחְבִּירָה,   וְהוּא אֶחָד וְאֵין שֵׁנִי,

וְלוֹ הָעֹז וְהַמִּשְׂרָה.   בְּלִי רֵאשִׁית, בְּלִי תַכְלִית,

וְצוּר חֶבְלִי בְּעֵת צָרָה,   וְהוּא אֵלִי וְחַי גּוֹאֲלִי,

מְנָת כּוֹסִי בְּיוֹם אֶקְרָא.   וְהוּא נִסִּי וּמָנוֹס לִי,

בְּעֵת אִישָׁן וְאָעִירָה,   בְּיָדוֹ אַפְקִיד רוּחִי,

יי לִי וְלֹא אִירָא.   וְעִם־רוּחִי גְּוִיָּתִי:

A-don o-lam a-sher ma-lach b'te-rem kol y'tzir niv-ra
l'eit na-a-sa v'chef-tzo kol, a-zai me-lech sh'mo nik-ra
V'a-cha-rei kich-lot ha-kol, l'va-do yim-loch no-ra,
ve-hu ha-ya ve-hu ho-veh, ve-hu yi-h'yeh b'tif-a-ra.
V'hu e-chad, v'ein shei-ni, l'ham-shil lo, l'hach-bi-ra,
b'li rei-sheet, b'li tach-lit, v'lo ha-oz v'ha-mis-ra.
V'hu Ei-li, v'chai go-a-li, v'tzur chev-li b'eit tza-ra,
v'hu ni-si u-ma-nos li, m'nat ko-si b'yom ek-ra.
B'ya-do af-kid ru-chi, b'eit i-shan v'a-i-ra,
v'im ru-chi g'vi-ya-ti: A-do-nai li, v'lo i-ra.

You are the Eternal, who reigned before any being had been created. When all was done according to Your will, already then, You were called Ruler.

And after all has ceased to be, still will You reign in solitary majesty; You were, are and will be in glory.

And You are my God, my living redeemer, my Rock in times of trouble and distress; You are my banner and my refuge, my benefactor when I call on You.

Into Your hands I entrust my spirit when I sleep and when I wake; and with my spirit my body also, the Eternal is with me, I will not fear.

94

EIN KEILOHEINU

אֵין כֵּאלֹהֵינוּ

אֵין כֵּאלֹהֵינוּ,
אֵין כְּמַלְכֵּנוּ,

מִי כֵאלֹהֵינוּ?
מִי כְמַלְכֵּנוּ?

נוֹדֶה לֵאלֹהֵינוּ,
נוֹדֶה לְמַלְכֵּנוּ,

בָּרוּךְ אֱלֹהֵינוּ,
בָּרוּךְ מַלְכֵּנוּ,

אַתָּה הוּא אֱלֹהֵינוּ,
אַתָּה הוּא מַלְכֵּנוּ,

אֵין כַּאדוֹנֵנוּ,
אֵין כְּמוֹשִׁיעֵנוּ.

מִי כַאדוֹנֵנוּ?
מִי כְמוֹשִׁיעֵנוּ?

נוֹדֶה לַאדוֹנֵנוּ,
נוֹדֶה לְמוֹשִׁיעֵנוּ.

בָּרוּךְ אֲדוֹנֵנוּ,
בָּרוּךְ מוֹשִׁיעֵנוּ.

אַתָּה הוּא אֲדוֹנֵנוּ,
אַתָּה הוּא מוֹשִׁיעֵנוּ.

Ein kei-lo-hei-nu, ein ka-do-nei-nu,
ein k'mal-kei-nu, ein k'mo-shi-ei-nu.

Mi chei-lo-hei-nu? Mi cha-do-nei-nu?
Mi ch'mal-kei-nu? Mi ch'mo-shi-ei-nu?

No-deh lei-lo-hei-nu, no-deh la-do-nei-nu,
no-deh l'mal-kei-nu, no-deh l'mo-shi-ei-nu.

Ba-ruch E-lo-hei-nu, ba-ruch A-do-nei-nu,
ba-ruch Mal-kei-nu, ba-ruch Mo-shi-ei-nu.

A-tah hu E-lo-hei-nu, a-tah hu A-do-nei-nu,
a-tah hu mal-kei-nu, a-tah hu Mo-shi-ei-nu.

There is none like our God, our Sovereign, our Redeemer.

Who is like our God, our Sovereign, our Redeemer?

We give thanks to our God, our Sovereign, our Redeemer.

Praised be our God, our Sovereign, our Redeemer.

You alone are our God, our Sovereign, our Redeemer.

יגדל

יִגְדַּל אֱלֹהִים חַי וְיִשְׁתַּבַּח, נִמְצָא וְאֵין עֵת אֶל־מְצִיאוּתוֹ.
אֶחָד וְאֵין יָחִיד כְּיִחוּדוֹ, נֶעְלָם וְגַם אֵין סוֹף לְאַחְדוּתוֹ.

אֵין לוֹ דְמוּת הַגּוּף וְאֵינוֹ גוּף, לֹא נַעֲרוֹךְ אֵלָיו קְדֻשָּׁתוֹ.
קַדְמוֹן לְכָל־דָּבָר אֲשֶׁר נִבְרָא, רִאשׁוֹן וְאֵין רֵאשִׁית
לְרֵאשִׁיתוֹ.

הִנּוֹ אֲדוֹן עוֹלָם, לְכָל־נוֹצָר, יוֹרֶה גְדֻלָּתוֹ וּמַלְכוּתוֹ.
שֶׁפַע נְבוּאָתוֹ נְתָנוֹ, אֶל־אַנְשֵׁי סְגֻלָּתוֹ וְתִפְאַרְתּוֹ.

לֹא קָם בְּיִשְׂרָאֵל כְּמֹשֶׁה עוֹד, נָבִיא וּמַבִּיט אֶת־תְּמוּנָתוֹ.
תּוֹרַת אֱמֶת נָתַן לְעַמּוֹ אֵל, עַל יַד נְבִיאוֹ נֶאֱמַן בֵּיתוֹ.

לֹא יַחֲלִיף הָאֵל, וְלֹא יָמִיר דָּתוֹ, לְעוֹלָמִים לְזוּלָתוֹ.
צוֹפֶה וְיוֹדֵעַ סְתָרֵינוּ, מַבִּיט לְסוֹף דָּבָר בְּקַדְמָתוֹ.

גּוֹמֵל לְאִישׁ חֶסֶד כְּמִפְעָלוֹ, נוֹתֵן לְרָשָׁע רַע כְּרִשְׁעָתוֹ.
יִשְׁלַח לְקֵץ יָמִין פְּדוּת עוֹלָם, כָּל־חַי וְיֵשׁ יַכִּיר יְשׁוּעָתוֹ.

חַיֵּי עוֹלָם נָטַע בְּתוֹכֵנוּ, בָּרוּךְ עֲדֵי עַד שֵׁם תְּהִלָּתוֹ.

Yig-dal Eh-lo-him chai v'yish-ta-bach, nim-tza v'ein eit el m'tzi-u-toh.
Eh-chad v'ein ya-chid k'yi-chu-do,
neh-lam v'gam ein sof l'ach-du-toh.

Ein lo d'mut ha-guf, v'ei-no guf, lo na-a-roch ei-lav k'du-sha-toh.
Kad-mon l'chol da-var a-sher niv-ra,
ri-shon v'ein rei-sheet l'rei-shee-toh.

Hi-no A-don o-lam l'chol no-tzar, yo-reh g'du-la-toh u-mal-chu-toh.
Sheh-fa n'vu-a-toh n'ta-no, el an-shei s'gu-la-toh v'tif-ar-toh.

Lo kam b'yis-ra-eil k'mo-sheh ohd, na-vi u-ma-bit et t'mu-na-toh,
To-rat eh-met na-tan l'a-mo Eil, al yad n'vi-o ne-eh-man bei-toh.

Lo ya-cha-lif ha-eil, v'lo ya-mir da-toh, l'o-la-mim l'zu-la-toh.
Tzo-feh v'yo-dei-a s'ta-rei-nu, ma-bit l'sof da-var b'kad-ma-toh.

Go-meil l'ish cheh-sed k'mif-a-lo, no-tein l'ra-sha ra k'rish-a-toh.
Yish-lach l'keitz ya-min p'dut o-lam,
kol chai v'yeish ya-kir y'shu-a-toh.

Cha-yei o-lam na-ta b'toh-chei-nu, ba-ruch a-dei ad sheim t'hi-la-toh.

Magnified be the living God, praised, whose existence is eternal, One and Unique in that unity, the unfathomable One whose Oneness is infinite.

A God with no bodily form, incorporeal, whose holiness is beyond compare, who preceded all creation, the Beginning who has no beginning!

You are Eternal Might, who teaches every creature Your greatness and sovereignty, with the gift of prophecy inspiring those to whom You choose to make Your glory known.

Never has there been a prophet like Moses, whose closeness to You is unmatched. A Torah of truth You have taught Your people through Your prophet, Your faithful servant.

A changeless God, ever the same, whose teaching will stand, who watches us and knows our inmost thoughts, who knows all outcomes before events begin!

You give us each what we deserve, the good and bad alike. In the end of days You will send an everlasting redemption; all that lives and has being shall witness Your deliverance.

You have implanted eternal life within us;
praised be Your glory to all eternity!

ESA EINAI   אשא עיני

אֶשָּׂא עֵינַי אֶל הֶהָרִים, מֵאַיִן יָבֹא עֶזְרִי.
עֶזְרִי מֵעִם יהוה, עֹשֵׂה שָׁמַיִם וָאָרֶץ.

E-sa ei-nai el heh-ha-rim, mei-ah-yin ya-voh ez-ri.
Ez-ri mei-im Adonai, o-seh sha-ma-yim va-a-retz.

I lift up my eyes unto the mountain,
From where does my help come?
My help comes from God.
Maker of heaven and earth.

EILI EILI

אלי, אלי

אֵלִי, אֵלִי,
שֶׁלֹא יִגָּמֵר לְעוֹלָם
הַחוֹל וְהַיָּם,
רִשְׁרוּשׁ שֶׁל הַמַּיִם,
בְּרַק הַשָּׁמַיִם,
תְּפִלַּת הָאָדָם.

Ei-li, Ei-li,
she-lo yi-ga-meir l'o-lam
ha-chol v'ha-yam
rish-rush shel ha-ma-yim,
b'rak ha-sha-ma-yim,
t'fi-lat ha-a-dam.

O God, O, my God,
I pray that these things never end:
The sand and the sea,
the rush of the waters,
the crash of the heavens,
the prayer of the heart.

KI ESHM'RA SHABBAT

כי אשמרה שבת

כִּי אֶשְׁמְרָה שַׁבָּת אֵל יִשְׁמְרֵנִי.
אוֹת הִיא לְעָלְמֵי עַד בֵּינוֹ וּבֵינִי.

Ki esh-m'ra sha-bat Eil yish-m'rei-ni.
Ot hi l'o-l'mei ad bei-no u-vei-ni.

As I observe Shabbat, God watches over me.
It is a sign for ever between God and me.

MA YAFEH HAYOM   מה יפה היום

מַה יָּפֶה הַיּוֹם, שַׁבָּת שָׁלוֹם.

Ma ya-feh ha-yom, Sha-bat sha-lom.

How beautiful this day is, Shabbat Shalom.

Y'DID NEFESH   ידיד נפש

יְדִיד נֶפֶשׁ, אָב הָרַחֲמָן, מְשׁוֹךְ עַבְדְּךָ אֶל רְצוֹנֶךָ.
יָרוּץ עַבְדְּךָ כְּמוֹ אַיָּל, יִשְׁתַּחֲוֶה אֶל מוּל הֲדָרֶךָ.

Y'did ne-fesh av ha-ra-cha-man,
m'shoch av-d'cha el r'tzo-ne-cha.
Ya-rutz av-d'cha k'mo a-yal
yish-ta-cha-veh
el mul ha-da-re-cha.

Heart's delight, Source of mercy, draw Your servant into Your arms.
I leap like a deer to stand in awe before You.

YOM ZEH L'YISAEIL   יום זה לישראל

יוֹם זֶה לְיִשְׂרָאֵל אוֹרָה וְשִׂמְחָה, שַׁבַּת מְנוּחָה.

Yom zeh l'yis-ra-eil o-ra v'sim-cha,
Sha-bat m'nu-cha.

This is Israel's day of light and joy, a Sabbath of rest.

T'FILAT HADERECH   תפלת הדרך

May we be blessed as we go on our way.
May we be guided in peace.
May we be blessed with health and joy.
May this be our blessing, Amen.

May we be sheltered by the wings of peace.
May we be kept in safety and in love.
May grace and compassion find their way to every soul.
May this be our blessing, Amen.

— Words by Debbie Friedman